Eucharistic
Devotion

Eucharistic Devotion

Renewing a Timeless Tradition

*Including Prayers for Visits
to the Blessed Sacrament*

A Redemptorist Pastoral Publication

Liguori
LIGUORI, MISSOURI

Imprimi Potest:
Richard Thibodeau, C.Ss.R.
Provincial, Denver Province
The Redemptorists

Imprimatur:
Most Reverend Michael J. Sheridan
Auxiliary Bishop, Archdiocese of St. Louis

Library of Congress Cataloging-in-Publication Data

Eucharistic devotion : renewing a timeless tradition / a Redemptorist pastoral publication.—Rev. ed.
      p. cm.
   ISBN 0-7648-0842-7 (pbk.)
   1. Lord's Supper (Liturgy). 2. Lord's Supper—Catholic Church. 3. Lord's Supper—Prayer-books and devotions—English. I. Redemptorists.

BX2215.3 .E93 2002
264'.36—dc21   2002016047

Copyright 1987, 2002, Liguori Publications
Printed in United States of America
05 04 03 02 01   5 4 3 2 1
Revised edition 2002

Contents

III. Fostering Eucharistic Devotions 31

IV. Eucharistic Prayers and Devotions 49

Introduction

The motive to write this book arose from a desire to support an authentic revival of those traditional eucharistic devotions that emphasize our Lord's presence flowing out from the celebration of the Mass into every dimension of our Christian life. Pope John Paul II in his encyclical letter, *"Redemptor Hominis,"* has this to say about the complementarity of the liturgical celebration of the Eucharist with eucharistic adoration: "Our communal worship at Mass must go together with our personal worship of Jesus in Eucharistic Adoration in order that our love may be complete."

By now, most people are thoroughly accustomed to the liturgical changes in the celebration of the Mass brought about by the Second Vatican Council, and they appreciate ongoing efforts to encourage active participation by all the faithful. But along with the renewed emphasis on the celebration of the Mass, many also experienced in their parishes or religious communities an almost total abandonment of the various forms of eucharistic veneration that previously meant so much to their spiritual growth. For example, many miss the observance of Forty Hours Devotion which, through the years, had become a highlight of enthusiastic participation in their parishes, sometimes resulting in unforgettable turning points in participants' lives of faith. This sense of loss is not based on mere sentimentalism; it is a result of sorrow in the face of a very real lack of something deemed necessary and needed.

Along with those members of the faithful whose memories include pre-Vatican II forms of eucharistic devotion are those who have never been introduced to authentic observances in honor of the Eucharist. Not only has the solemn exposition of the Blessed Sacrament and its solemn blessing seemingly been abandoned, but many lay persons, priests, and religious in some parts of the Catholic world seem to have given up their visits to the Blessed Sacrament and seem not to feel the need or miss the joy of responding to the Lord's gracious permanent presence in the tabernacle.

People become even more confused when they adopt the wrong impression that the Holy See and the Second Vatican Council actually intended to abolish these forms of eucharistic devotion. In 1965, in full agreement with the Council, Pope Paul VI emphasized in his encyclical, *Mystery of Faith ("Mysterium Fidei"),* the real and permanent presence of the Lord in the Eucharist and pointed out the importance of devotions that surround the reservation of the Eucharist. In May 1967, the Holy See issued a document entitled *Instruction on Eucharistic Worship ("Eucharisticum Mysterium"),* which helped Catholics to better understand the history of the Eucharist and the deeper meanings of its devotional forms. In June 1973, instructions for the liturgical rites of eucharistic adoration and celebration were published in *The Roman Ritual: Holy Communion and Worship of the Eucharist Outside Mass.* And with the same purpose in mind—to promote a sound revival of eucharistic veneration—Pope John Paul II published, in 1980, his letter to all bishops, *On the Mystery and Worship of the Eucharist ("Dominicae Cenae").* Finally, in 1993, the U.S. bishops published a collection of rites and texts for use by those in charge of the celebration of the exposition of the Eucharist entitled *Order for the Solemn Exposition of the Holy Eucharist.*

Based on these documents and on notable studies of the history, theology, and spirituality of eucharistic worship, these pages are written to encourage those who have persevered in practicing their beloved eucharistic devotions with enthusiasm and to open new doors to those who have somehow missed an introduction to these venerable and uplifting forms of prayer. It is also hoped that those who are now participating in a revival of these eucharistic devotions, consonant, of course, with their authentic observance, will learn from this book a better understanding of the history and the profound meaning of the various forms of eucharistic devotions.

Those priests who serve as military or hospital chaplains— those who care for wounded and dying people, military and civilian—have reason to know the immense consolation that people gain from the opportunity to receive Holy Communion when they are in danger or near death. Truly they know, firsthand, the comfort and solace provided by Jesus in the form of the eucharistic species—our Way, our Life, and the Consoler of the sick and dying.

Also, as members of the Redemptorist family, priests, brothers, and laity, sons and daughters of Saint Alphonsus, one of the great venerators of the Blessed Sacrament, we acknowledge our desire to perpetuate his great vision of eucharistic devotion as a significant constituent of the Christian life.

The Lord can never be praised enough for his great testament, the Eucharist, and his abiding presence among us. We join the angels and saints in their unending worship. And we hope that these pages will inspire each reader to make his or her life an expression of enduring eucharistic praise.

ONE

History of Eucharistic Devotion

Holy Scripture provides us with ample evidence of the Eucharist as the Lord's testament, as memorial, as sign of abiding presence, source of life eternal, sign of unity, and proclamation of Christ's death and Resurrection until he comes again in glory. As for devotions founded on Christ's eucharistic presence, the history of the Church gives us pertinent information, and the teaching authority of the Church provides guidance for present practice in this area. Here we will consider the history of the eucharistic celebration and especially the devotions which developed as a result of our Lord's presence on the altar.

The Mass:
Center and Summit
of Christian Community

The teaching of the Church provides abundant evidence that the celebration of the eucharistic memorial—as sacrifice and meal—is absolutely vital for the life of the Church and particularly for all the other forms of eucharistic devotion.

The *Constitution on the Sacred Liturgy* and the postconciliar liturgical renewal have brought this home to all the faithful. This renewal has also furthered the ecumenical movement, since the Eastern Orthodox churches and the ecclesiastical communities born of the sixteenth-century Reformation were extremely critical about certain forms of the eucharistic cult. Both the Eastern Orthodox and Protestant Churches felt that Catholic liturgical practice had become unfaithful to the biblical doctrine on the Eucharist, particularly overemphasizing eucharistic devotions to the detriment of the eucharistic celebration of the Lord's Supper.

Most expressions of eucharistic worship, as they were known at the time of the Second Vatican Council, were not practiced during the first thousand years of the Church. When new forms developed in and after the eleventh century, the Church authorities consistently rejected any practice that might overshadow the centrality of the eucharistic celebration as such. From the eleventh to the thirteenth centuries, the practice of distributing Communion outside the eucharistic celebration was introduced in many parts of the Western Church. This new practice was often censured but later tolerated only as an exception. Good theology explained Communion outside Mass to be in conformity with the ancient Christian practice.

From the earliest times, there were many cases of reception of Communion outside the direct celebration of the Mass. During the first centuries, the faithful could bring Holy Communion to the sick, especially to the dying, but also to others who were unable to participate in the celebration of Mass. It was clearly understood, however, that this practice was meant to bring them a share of the eucharistic memorial, the great sign of unity. Thus, those who received the eucharistic species at home felt included in the eucharistic sacrifice. We shall see later that, already during the first centuries, there were exceptions. Especially in times of persecution, the faithful could keep the reserved species in their homes for several days.

The history of the Eucharist records many innovations which, however, did not survive. One of the best documented practices of this kind was an effort to emphasize the unity of all parishes with the bishop or the unity of bishops with the successor of Peter. Innocent I, in 416, writes in a letter to Bishop Decentius of Gubbio about the practice of *fermentum*: immediately after the Mass celebrated by the bishop of Rome, acolytes were to bring consecrated species to the churches in the neighborhood, not for reservation but for use at the moment when, during the Mass, the consecrated bread is mixed with the consecrated wine. The *fermentum* was distributed only five times a year: on Thursday and Saturday of Holy Week, and on Easter, Pentecost, and Christmas.

During the eighth century, the pope gave to each newly consecrated bishop the eucharistic bread from which he could receive Communion during the following forty days. Bishops in France did the same for the newly ordained priests. These priests celebrated their own Mass but mixed the *fermentum* into the consecrated species during the celebration as a sign of unity with the bishop. However, these practices never became universal, and they eventually died out. Although they in no way opposed the centrality of the eucharistic celebration as such—since they were meant only to emphasize unity in the celebration—they were, in the eyes of many, inappropriate expressions.

Reservation of the Eucharist: Viaticum and Communion for the Sick

The most ancient, best documented, and most relevant forms of reservation of the eucharistic species were the Viaticum and Communion for the sick. The word "viaticum" is from the Latin, meaning "food for the journey," and refers to the reception of Holy Communion by a dying person as a spiritual aid in the passage from death into eternal life. This practice provides the most evident testimony of faith in the permanent presence of the Lord in the consecrated Host and provides the most convincing argument for the reservation of the consecrated species.

The oldest form of Viaticum is the "home Communion," where there was either a Mass in the sick person's house or—more commonly—a member of the family or another lay person brought the consecrated Host directly from the eucharistic celebration to the sufferer. During a long period of history, the consecrated species could be preserved in the home of a gravely sick person so that he or she could receive Communion, especially on the last day or hour of life. From the fourth century on, however, the more common practice was to bring or send the Viaticum directly from the eucharistic celebration or to distribute it within a home Mass. Later, in many places, a few eucharistic species were preserved in the sanctuary, in the sacristy, or in the priest's house—to be used for emergency sick calls.

From the eleventh century onward, the solemn rite of Viaticum developed more and more into a distinct observance. The one who carried the Viaticum was often joined by a pious procession of many people. We shall return later to the many ways in which the Church, throughout the ages, strove to make sure that Viaticum was available for all the faithful. Here we witness a most moving dimension of eucharistic devotion: welcoming, revering, and loving the divine Visitor on its journey to the sick and dying.

The Eucharist: Companion on Journeys and in Times of Distress

Jesus assures us that if we trust in him he will accompany us on our journey in this valley of tears. From this assurance, many Christians drew the conclusion that they acted in accord with Jesus' intentions when they kept with them the eucharistic species on long and dangerous journeys. The consecrated bread, which they hung around their necks in a special casket, served as a safeguard for the journey and provided assurance of receiving the Viaticum if they were in danger of death. There are only a few documents from the fourth to the eighth centuries about this custom, but such a practice at that time was not astonishing since preservation of the Eucharist by the laity was not yet universally forbidden. In the Eastern Churches, hermits and stylites were allowed to have the Eucharist with them as their permanent "companion" and thus have it available as their Viaticum in their final hour.

Throughout the Middle Ages, it was not unusual, during Crusades and on the battlefield, for a priest—even at the front—to carry the Body of Christ. But there was never a universal law allowing or encouraging the practice.

From the fourteenth to the eighteenth centuries, several popes when journeying took the Eucharist with them in solemn procession. The pope, riding in his carriage, was preceded by a white horse carrying on his back a tabernacle which held the consecrated wafer. In this case, the motivation for this practice was quite different. The custom was influenced by the Corpus Christi procession, with the pope coming "in the name of the Lord." Benedict XIII seems to be the last pope who conducted his journeys in this way.

There is also an old tradition which, indeed, has never died out. During times of persecution of Christians, the Eucharist was sent to those in prison. Those in danger of death (martyrs-to-be) also were allowed to have the consecrated Host with them. And there are moving accounts of people taking extreme risks to bring the eucharistic Host to those imprisoned in concentration camps during our own century.

Further Development of Eucharistic Devotion

No learned Protestant theologian would maintain what sixteenth-century Protestant reformers asserted: They condemned any form of eucharistic devotion—other than the Lord's Supper itself—as idolatry. It is true that the first eleven or twelve centuries of Church history reveal only traces of these devotions. But there was a gradual development of eucharistic devotion over time. Numerous documents from the first centuries indicate a great reverence for our Lord's presence in the Eucharist, even though it was not reserved in a tabernacle for adoration.

During those first centuries when the laity were allowed to bring the eucharistic Host to their homes and to reserve it there for the sick or for daily Communion, there was always a great emphasis on reverence, on adoration of the Lord as he was received in Communion, and on great care for the safety of the consecrated species.

Throughout the ages, however, tension did develop in different areas over proper care for the safety of the Host, and for responsible manifestation of reverence. Furthermore, there was not always and everywhere unanimous agreement on what reverence required or allowed. For instance, in some parts of the East, the conviction prevailed that reverence for the Lord's sacramental presence required that if some consecrated Hosts remained after being brought from Mass as Viaticum, they should be burned or buried in the earth. However, other voices in the Church maintained that this procedure manifested irreverence. The latter opinion finally prevailed everywhere.

Until the ninth century, during times of persecution and even during peaceful times, in some sectors of the Church, the eucharistic Host was entrusted to the laity and reserved in private homes. Later, only clergy—normally priests—were responsible for this custody, and only very few consecrated species were allowed to be reserved for Viaticum. It was not until centuries later that the sacrament was reserved for distribution outside the Mass and explicitly for the greater devotion of the worshipers.

For a long time, the Eucharist was reserved either in the priest's house or in the sacristy or in some other place where it could be protected. Here the emphasis was evidently on safety—to prevent attempts at sacrilegious abuse. The tension between concern for the safety of the reserved Eucharist and easy access to Jesus' sacramental presence for the people has continued down through the ages. Many Catholics, for example, are disappointed when a parish church is locked almost all day, even though common sense, in particular instances, may dictate that this is a necessary precaution. However, while knowledge of the history does not remove a feeling of disappointment, it does make for a greater tolerance and mutual understanding.

During the tenth century, the Eucharist was usually reserved in the sacristy. However, when public veneration of the Blessed Sacrament increased in many parts of the Church in the eleventh century, the privileged place of reservation gradually came to be an ornamental cubicle in the main church. Later on, this tabernacle received ever more artistic attention, although in Italy, for a long time, the sacristy remained the preferred place of reservation; in Milan, because of the influence of Saint Charles Borromeo, this was so until the latter part of the fifteenth century.

Many churches had beautiful sacrament-chapels with ornate tabernacles. The altar-tabernacle, at least in the sense of the tabernacle placed on the main altar, was an exception until much later. And in many cases, Church legislation discouraged reservation of the Hosts on the main altar, where the eucharistic sacrifice was usually celebrated. This prohibition was issued, however, not to oppose eucharistic devotion or to discourage adoration of the Blessed Sacrament in silent prayer nor did the reasoning center on safety, but rather it hinged on the fact that the altar is the place of eucharistic sacrifice. In Rome, this tradition was very strong. There was never a tabernacle on the main altar, especially in the great papal basilicas. There were, and still are, beautiful sacrament-chapels within the basilicas, however.

Some still may remember the former rules of fast before Holy Communion. These dated back to the third century and were probably introduced even earlier. The legal prescriptions underwent many changes and sometimes caused undue scrupulosity. Young priests of a different generation frequently had to observe complete fasting until afternoon, after hearing confessions and celebrating Mass in various places. This practice of fasting was, among other things, a reminder to look forward to the great moment of Holy Communion. But the change in regulation was timely. For example, missionary and native-born priests in Africa, under the rigid fasting legislation, could celebrate Mass only in the early morning because their health would have suffered terribly if, in the hot climate, they could not have taken water during the day.

Eucharistic Devotion
From the Eleventh Century Onward

It is a puzzling fact that, in spite of the firm faith in the permanent presence of the Lord in the consecrated species, and in spite of the great reverence evoked by it in the first ten centuries, there was no noticeable development of a public eucharistic rite outside the celebration of the eucharistic memorial. Beginning in the eleventh century, certain forms of eucharistic piety and cult began to develop, but for several centuries the main reason given for reservation of the Blessed Sacrament was only its use as the Viaticum. For example, as late as 1346, a synod in Florence speaks only of the Viaticum as reason for reserving the sacrament. And the statutes of

Bishop Wenceslaus in Breslau, in 1410, forbade, except on the feast of Corpus Christi, the reservation of the Blessed Sacrament for any reason other than Communion for the sick.

Instructions from the Holy See in 1949 and in 1967 followed the ancient tradition, indicating that the main reason for the reservation of the Blessed Sacrament was its use as Viaticum. But this stated purpose was and is no reason to belittle other reasons, such as people's fervent prayer and adoration before the tabernacle.

The introduction in the thirteenth century of the elevation of the Host at Mass after the consecration and before the Our Father brought on further development of eucharistic worship. The faithful took to heart the words of the psalmist, "my eyes are turning toward the Lord," and were thus led to a deep and fervent cult of adoration. Many people began to experience great consolation during this exposition of the Blessed Sacrament at Mass. In fact, in some cases, a black velvet backdrop was erected so that the faithful could get a better view of the consecrated Host; and great care was taken not to let the smoke from the incense block the sight of the Host from the faithful.

Great saints, such as Bernard of Clairvaux and Francis of Assisi, were tireless promoters of eucharistic devotion in its various forms. In 1209, Juliana of Mont-Cornillon, a pious nun of Liège, began to promote the liturgical celebration of the feast of Corpus Christi. It was officially celebrated for the first time at Liège in 1247, and in 1264 it was given formal approval by Pope Urban IV. A main feature of the feast since the fourteenth century has been a eucharistic procession which may take place on or near the feast day itself.

TWO

Main Dimensions of the Mass, Our Eucharistic Memorial

In our study of the history of the Eucharist and eucharistic devotion, from its early beginnings until the present, one of the most evident facts is the centrality and normative value of the eucharistic memorial, the Mass. Therefore, before reflecting on the various forms of eucharistic devotion outside of the Mass, we must look first to the main dimensions of the Eucharist itself.

First of all, it is the memorial which Christ gave us on the eve of his death when he said, "Do this in memory of me." It is the solemn assurance of his abiding, life-giving presence—"I shall be with you"—bringing us into intimate contact with his saving sacrifice: "This is my body given for you, my blood shed for you." It provides a redeeming entrance into the company of the "Lamb of God" who destroys the vicious circle of violence, enmity, and treachery. It is a covenantal sharing: "This is the cup of my blood, the blood of the new and everlasting covenant." It emphasizes the importance of conversion: "So that sins may be forgiven." It is the "mystery of faith" which enkindles in us a joyful, grateful faith, and builds up the faith community: "Every time you eat this bread and drink this cup you proclaim the death of the Lord until he comes." And finally, the Eucharist has the power to make us, in Christ, "adorers in spirit and in truth."

"Do This in Memory of Me"

The Eucharist is a most distinctive memorial. Recalling the greatest event of God's self-revealing and self-giving love, we praise the Lord, who most graciously remembers us. He calls for our grateful memory of him.

By the eucharistic testament given to his disciples, Jesus assures us that he will always remember us and wants to be with us whenever, as a community of disciples, we gather to remember his death and Resurrection. By this one-of-a-kind memorial, he teaches us the relevance of memory, brings our faulty human memory up to the level of a eucharistic one, filled with grateful recollection of all of God's saving works, all his gifts, and all his promises.

The eucharistic memorial is not just a onetime human effort to recall an event. It is the Lord himself who, by his powerful presence, reminds us that the love with which he gave himself up on the Cross is solemnly guaranteed by his eucharistic testament. This enactment of great power and purpose calls for a most generous response on our part.

While God assures us that he will always be gracious and keep his promise of mercy, he sends us his Spirit to ensure that each member of the community remembers in the proper way. The memorial is rightly celebrated when we learn to remember and to celebrate the entire history of salvation, all the works of God, in the focal light of the death and Resurrection of Christ who, by this very memorial, makes us sharers in the event and in the fruits of his Paschal Mystery.

This right understanding brings us to a new vision, a new appreciation of the Incarnation of the Word of God, of Jesus' life, and of all that happened to his flock since his death, Resurrection, and Ascension into heaven. The lives of Christians who, day by day, relive gratefully the history of salvation—through a eucharistic memory—give clear evidence of this fact which gives cohesion and coherence to their way of life.

Through the eucharistic memorial, Jesus reminds us that, in the name of all the redeemed, he is present forever to the Father as total gift of himself, pleading for us; and at the same time he is present to us, always ready to give the wonderful gift of himself. Our capacity to receive Christ as total gift depends mainly on the quality of our memory. Is it a healthy, grateful memory or an impoverished one? The Divine Healer makes himself present in the memorial also to heal what we remember. We cannot make a generous and loving response unless we develop a thankful and forgiving memory. Furthermore, we cannot tune in on the wavelength of this wonderful memorial unless we long to respond to the self-giving love of Jesus by our own grateful response, entrusting ourselves entirely to him.

The eucharistic memorial leads to all-encompassing thanksgiving. Rendering thanks, Jesus takes the bread, saying, "Take this, all of you, and eat it: this is my body...." And again he says of the wine: "This is the cup of my blood...." The changing of bread and wine into his body and blood recalls the fact that Jesus was truly God. The eucharistic species remind us that bread and wine are gifts of the Creator, given us anew by our Redeemer. "Blessed are you, Lord, God of all creation. Through your goodness we have this bread to offer...this wine to offer...."

If we have a truly eucharistic memory whereby we relive the Paschal Mystery, we have also a new, redeemed perception of the bread and wine. They stand for all the gifts of creation, and we honor them as God's gifts, given for all. This way of looking at the eucharistic sharing of God's gifts provides us with a new insight into the manner we earn our "bread," or income, in daily life.

"I Shall Be With You"

The Eucharist is the most remarkable manifestation of Jesus' *advent* and *presence* in our midst. It is, therefore, important that we understand the specific aspects and dimensions of this presence. It is absolutely real, even more real than our personal presence to one another here on earth.

On the Cross, Jesus is signally present to his Father, entrusting himself to the Father, knowing that he is the acceptable offering. He is really present to his Mother, who stands beneath the Cross. He reaches out to her with strong and tender love, addressing her, entrusting her to his beloved disciple and, indeed, entrusting all of us to her. He is present in an astonishing way to the criminal crucified with him, assuring him of everlasting presence in paradise. And he is present to those who, by their sins, have crucified him: "Father, forgive!" All this is proof of his compelling presence, empowered by the Holy Spirit, who enables and anoints him to be with us as total gift of himself.

Jesus' presence in the eucharistic memorial matches perfectly his sacrificial presence on the Cross. It vividly manifests his sacrificial presence in the Paschal Mystery. In a special way, it is the presence of Jesus' sacrificial love for us. He stands before the Father as the acceptable sacrifice, interceding for us.

He is with us in his heavenly fullness, in the final glory of his all-embracing, self-giving love, although in a sacramentally indicated and hidden form. Through this sacramental presence, Jesus affirms that he died for us, continues to live for us in the present, and will be with us forever. His presence as an abiding gift is a great challenge—a challenge for us to respond by giving ourselves to him as freely as he offered himself on the Cross.

But his presence offers us infinitely more than a mere moral challenge. To those who believe in him he offers the power of the Holy Spirit, who grants them the courage to give themselves as total gift to Jesus and, with him, to the Father. Thus, they share actively in Jesus' and the Father's love for all their brothers and sisters. The Eucharist also offers a new range of vision for viewing our own human presence—our being with and for one another.

The real presence of the eucharistic Lord is directly connected with his sacrifice. Jesus' presence is absolute and unconditional, but our response depends on the degree to which we are actually present to him and to one another in a sacrificial love, ready to renounce whatever hinders and undermines such a love.

The divine presence of Jesus is realized in the established

realm of love to which only the loving belong. He is our ultimate destiny. By permitting the Holy Spirit to shape our
memory into a truly grateful one in this memorial, we allow
the Spirit to make us into an acceptable gift in return for
Jesus' presence throughout our lives. His presence brings with
it the life-giving Spirit. Those who refuse the gift and challenge of this life-giving Spirit cut themselves off from the saving presence of the eucharistic Lord.

In the eucharistic memorial, the Church, by the power of
the Holy Spirit, places on the altar the sacramental signs of
the sacrifice of Christ, knowing that the Father endorses Jesus'
redemptive love. The real presence of Jesus in the Eucharist
reminds us of what he did for us and what he is for us.

By positioning sacramentally on the altar the Lamb who
died for us and who stands before the Father rendering thanks,
praising, and interceding for us all, the Church emphasizes
the Trinitarian reality of the eucharistic presence. By the power
of the Holy Spirit, and with Christ and the Father, she sends
her love out into the world. She encourages people to open
themselves to this vision and to do away with everything that
stands in the way of this kind of being-present—a presence
in loving obedience to the Father, who wants all his children
to be truly alive to him in mutual manifestation of Christlike
love for one another.

The real presence of the risen Lord in the Eucharist is a
mystery calling for reverence, awe, and adoration; it is not
capable of any kind of philosophical "explanation." Yet, for
the believer, the vital dimensions of this eucharistic presence
can be examined in view of challenge and response.

1. The concept of Real Presence implies personal communication. Christ's presence in the Eucharist points to the most

sublime communication and, above all, to *Communion.* It involves the Church and each believing participant in a loving communication with the Father. Through Communion, we are ushered into the mutual love between the Father and the Incarnate Son in the power of the Holy Spirit. The Spirit not only communicates to us the powerful message that Christ died for us but also makes us sharers in his love so that, in Christ, we can love God with God's love and love one another with the Father's love and with Christ's love as well.

2. The glorified Christ is with the Father, *in his glory as God-Man.* He comes to us in the Eucharist and abides with us in order to lead us finally into the same presence *in the glory of the Father.* Jesus' presence is dynamic, powerfully shaping our final presence, our final home in God.

3. Christ has chosen bread and wine as sacramental signs for his nourishing presence, thereby implying to his Church and his disciples that he himself is the nourishing love and presence on our pilgrim way. He also empowers us to become effective signs of nourishing love for one another in human and spiritual needs.

God's real presence, meant to nourish a person's faith, hope, and love, calls for self-examination on the part of the recipient. It is a great challenge. Everyone must "examine" themselves before eating a share of the bread and drinking from the cup (1 Cor 11:28). Those who "eat of the bread" while refusing true faith and love are desecrating the real presence of Jesus, and are condemned to exile from him.

4. Christ is present on earth in this distinctive way by the *epiclesis,* the Church's calling on the power of the Holy Spirit before, during, and after the words by which Jesus instituted

the eucharistic memorial. The Spirit (through this liturgical invocation) descends upon the offering—the bread and wine—at the time of the consecration, to make them signs of Jesus' life-giving presence. The Church also calls the Holy Spirit to come upon the participants so that, in a spirit of generous response, they may be in communion with the Lord and in communication with one another.

5. Christ is present to nourish his Church, to build up his mystical body in unity, love, and solidarity. We make a genuine response if we long to become constructive members of Christ's body, the Church.

"This Is My Body Given for You, My Blood Shed for You"

The very words of the institution of the Eucharist turn our attention to the sacrifice wherein Christ, on the Cross, offered himself for our salvation. The memorial, celebrated in the form of a meal, is a sharing in the death that Christ suffered for us and an entering into his sacrificing, reconciling love.

Authorized by Christ himself and in the power of the Holy Spirit, the Church proclaims the death and Resurrection of Christ. She is assured, and assures her believers, that Christ gives himself at Communion with the same love that he manifested by his death on the Cross. We praise him for that abiding, life-giving love by being ready to put to death in ourselves whatever might be an obstacle to the same kind of love. It is inconceivable that we could participate in the sacrifice of praise without being ready to conquer in ourselves the poisoning powers of selfishness, violence, pride, and arrogance. With the whole Church we pray to God, in the eucharistic memorial, to help us to appreciate ever more his work of redemption and to relive the Paschal Mystery of his cruel death and glorious Resurrection for the salvation of the world.

Eucharistic veneration, in all its dimensions and aspects, turns our grateful attention to the Cross to enable us, by faith in the Resurrection, to bear our burdens in the same spirit as Christ bore his Cross for us. The sacrificial death— into which we enter by Communion—and the whole eucharistic celebration involve no physical death; but this memorial sets in motion the ongoing process of putting to death any selfish and sensual tendencies. At the same time, it also reminds us of the hour of our own death and gives us the courage and strength to unite our dying with the redeeming death of Christ, and to rejoice in the hope of resurrection.

As fruit of the eucharistic sacrifice and of Communion with the body of Christ scourged for us and the blood of Christ shed for us, we can say with Saint Paul: "I am now rejoicing in my sufferings for your sake, and in my flesh I am completing what is lacking in Christ's afflictions for the sake of his body, that is, the church. I became its servant according to God's commission that was given to me for you, to make the word of God fully known, the mystery that has been hidden throughout the ages and generations but has now been revealed to his saints" (Col 1:24–26).

"Lamb of God, You Take Away the Sins of the World"

A dimension of the Eucharist and of all forms of eucharistic worship that deserves particular attention is indicated by the prayer, "Lamb of God, you take away the sins of the world: have mercy on us...grant us peace."

This prayer reminds us not so much of the Paschal lamb of the Exodus when the Passover was instituted (Ex 12) as of the songs of the Servant and his peace mission:

> *Surely he has borne our infirmities*
> *and carried our diseases;*
> *yet we accounted him stricken,*
> *struck down by God, and*
> *afflicted.*
> *But he was wounded for our*
> *transgressions,*
> *crushed for our iniquities;*
> *upon him was the punishment*
> *that made us whole,*
> *and by his bruises we are*
> *healed.*
> *All we like sheep have gone astray;*
> *we have all turned to our own*
> *way.*
> *and the* LORD *has laid on him*
> *the iniquity of us all.*
>
> *He was oppressed, and he was*
> *afflicted,*
> *yet he did not open his mouth;*
> *like a lamb that is led to the*
> *slaughter,*
> *and like a sheep that before its*
> *shearers is silent,*
> *so he did not open his mouth....*

They made his grave with the
     wicked
   and his tomb with the rich,
although he had done no
     violence,
   and there was no deceit in his
     mouth.

Yet it was the will of the LORD
   to crush him with pain.
When you make his life an
     offering for sin,
   he shall see his offspring, and
     shall prolong his days;
through him the will of the LORD
     shall prosper....
Therefore I will allot him a
     portion with the great,
   and he shall divide the spoil
     with the strong:
because he poured out himself
     to death,
   and was numbered with
     the transgressors;
yet he bore the sin of many,
   and made intercession for the
     transgressors.
     ISAIAH 53:4–7, 9–10, 12

The New Testament leaves no doubt that Jesus was and understood himself explicitly to be that Servant of whom the four songs speak: the Servant who suffers like a lamb and by his gentleness breaks the deadly circle of violence. He bears the horrifying burden of the world's transgressions, and opens the way for a saving solidarity and peace. At the baptism of Jesus in the Jordan, "a voice from heaven said, 'This is my Son, the Beloved, with whom I am well pleased'" (Mt 3:17). These words clearly point to the first verse of the first song of the Servant (Isa 42:1). And it is John the Baptizer who points to Jesus, saying: "Here is the Lamb of God who takes away the sin of the world" (Jn 1:29).

The whole eucharistic memorial exhorts us to "behold the Lamb of God!" It urges us to learn from him who is meek, nonviolent, humble, and thus points out the way of peace. The Lamb "standing as if it had been slaughtered" (Rev 5:6) is "worthy to take the scroll / and to open its seals" (Rev 5:9) to reveal the deepest meaning of the history of salvation. The Eucharist brings the pilgrim Church into the heavenly liturgy: "Salvation belongs to our God / who is seated on the / throne, and to the Lamb" (Rev 7:10). The Lamb of God turns our eyes and hearts to his ways of loving forgiveness. He rescues even his enemies, the sinners, by his life and death; he shows us the healing power of nonviolence as the expression of redeeming love for those who oppose him and his disciples.

The deepest meaning of Christ's sin-offering, which we celebrate in the Eucharist, is not the payment of a debt imposed by vindictive justice but, rather, the bearing of the burden of all sinners; it is thus a call to total conversion. He, alone, in whom there is no violence and no treachery, can deliver us from the solidarity of sin and lead us into the solidarity of salvation.

Devotion to the Eucharist should open our eyes to the Redeemer's nonviolence and, particularly, to nonviolence as the healing response to humanity's present madness, which claims that the mutual threat of total annihilation is the way to peace. The Eucharist does not present ready solutions to the terrible problems caused by the arms race of the super-powers and their satellites. But we can learn much about peace by listening with our hearts to the Lamb of God whose final victory we celebrate in the Eucharist. By his body given for us and his blood shed for us, we develop an effective love for all our neighbors and especially for those who are enemies of patient nonviolence and absolute truthfulness.

"This Is the Cup of My Blood, the Blood of the New and Everlasting Covenant"

By shedding his own blood, not that of others or of scape-goats (as in Old Testament sacrifices), Jesus seals the new and everlasting covenant of a saving solidarity. Sharing in Christ's body given for us and his blood shed for us, we enter into this covenant expressed by a love that will never become disordered.

Saint Augustine, time and again, wrote of his tremendous vision: to receive the body of Christ and become the body of Christ—a fitting member, a supportive member, ready to make all the sacrifices needed for keeping and fostering the bonds of unity and peace. When we share faithfully in the cup of the new covenant, we endorse the "law of Christ" written in our hearts: "Bear one another's burdens, and in this way you will fulfill the law of Christ" (Gal 6:2).

Eucharistic worship is authentic if all our thinking and all our human relationships confirm our membership in this community of salvation. It is unthinkable to live a covenant solidarity only on the level of devotion. We, who receive in the Eucharist the Word of God and the body and blood of Christ as signs of redemption, must show a redeemed attitude in dealing with earthly goods. Christians of wealthy industrial nations will prove that they have benefitted from eucharistic worship when they begin to recognize that unfair appropriation of resources is often the cause of many national and international socioeconomic problems.

Sharing on all levels is, in a certain sense, a "natural" action for Christians who know what they receive and what they celebrate in the Eucharist.

"So That Sins May Be Forgiven"

There are many avenues of divine forgiveness, liturgical and extra-liturgical. In the first place there is baptism. "'Repent,' said Peter, 'and be baptized every one of you in the name of Jesus Christ so that your sins may be forgiven'" (Acts 2:38). There is also a dimension of forgiveness of sins in the sacrament of the anointing of the sick. "Are any among you suffering?...They should call for the elders of the church and have them pray over them, anointing them with oil in the name of the Lord. The prayer of faith will save the sick, and the Lord will raise them up; and anyone who has committed sins will be forgiven. Therefore confess your sins to one another, and pray for one another, so that you may be healed. The prayer of the righteous is powerful and effective" (Jas 5:13–16). James's text on the anointing of the sick is also preceded by a strong warning: "Do not grumble against one another, so that you may not be judged" (Jas 5:9).

All sacramental and nonsacramental ways of obtaining forgiveness of sins from God imply the condition expressed in the Lord's prayer: "Forgive us our trespasses as we forgive those who trespass against us." The forgiveness and reconciliation offered graciously by God call for total reconciliation: peace with God, with individuals, and among nations. Forgiveness finds its center in the Paschal Mystery of Christ's death and Resurrection, which we celebrate in the eucharistic memorial; it is this celebration which introduces us ever more completely to God's love. We listen to Jesus' prayer on the Cross, offered for all of us: "Father, forgive." From these words, the healing power of the gospel of peace and reconciliation emanate. And from them we learn the gentle "law of grace," whereby we meet one another in healing, forgiving love—especially those who, by their enmity and violence, are in special need of such love and reconciliation.

Our access to the saving and healing dimension of the Eucharist reminds us how much we need the ministrations of healing, forgiving grace. "If we say that we have no sin, we deceive ourselves, and the truth is not in us. If we confess our sins, he who is faithful and just will forgive us our sins and cleanse us from all unrighteousness. If we say that we have not sinned, we make him a liar, and his word is not in us" (1 Jn 1:8–10).

The entire eucharistic liturgy reminds us of our need to be forgiven and the importance of starting life anew. Right at the beginning we confess our sins as a group. Then the proclamation of the Word of God and the priest's homily serve to make us more aware of our need to be more open to God's healing forgiveness.

During the early centuries, in many areas of the Church, the first part of Mass provided a time for general confession of sins and general absolution. But those who had committed gravely scandalous sins were not allowed to receive Communion without previous reconciliation through the sacrament of penance. The Communion rite has no less than three prayers that focus on forgiveness: the "Our Father," "Deliver us, Lord, from every evil" (marking sin as the greatest evil), and "Lamb of God, you take away the sins the world: have mercy on us." Then, before receiving Communion we humbly acknowledge once more our need for healing forgiveness: "Lord, I am not worthy...."

All these prayers seeking forgiveness together with readiness to forgive one another as the Lord God forgives us are brought into the realm of the Eucharist: to praise and thank God for his healing action in Christ, our Redeemer, and to thank Jesus who gave himself up for us "so that we may be forgiven." Thus, the Eucharist enkindles in us that love of God and neighbor that banishes fear and erases sin.

"Mystery of Faith"

The Eucharist is the summit of our religious existence. The whole life of the Church derives from it and leads to it. Above all, it is the supreme expression and celebration of the Church's faith, the precious "sacrament of faith," through which the faith of the community nourishes and strengthens the faith of each participant. It is and should be an ever more joyous, grateful celebration of faith, filled with hope which in turn bears fruit in love for the life of the world.

In the Eucharist, the Lord feeds us with his Word, meditated on and celebrated by the community of faith, in preparation for nourishment with the Lord's body and blood. Both his Word and his Body are the bread from heaven which can bring us to the fullness of faith and a life worthy of the children of God. This point has great ecumenical relevance. The

Second Vatican Council's liturgical renewal—especially the use of the vernacular for the proclamation of the Word of God—has torn down many barriers between Catholics and people of other faiths who desire to understand our faith in the Eucharist in its various dimensions.

The evident vitality exhibited by a Christian community celebrating "the mystery of faith" is definite proof of the excellence of the Eucharist. This fact has been proven time and again.

While the eucharistic celebration is the summit and fruitful source of a life of faith active in love, the various forms of sound eucharistic devotions other than the Mass itself are also highly relevant for deepening and strengthening faith.

"Every Time You Eat This Bread and Drink This Cup, You Proclaim the Death of the Lord, Until He Comes"

Christ can be present in all the Masses celebrated throughout the world because he is in the glory of the Father. He has attained his final purpose and destiny. The Lamb, slaughtered as an offering for our sins, fulfills the saving plan to reconcile the universe through his death and reigns forever over heaven and earth. In him, all of redeemed humanity and, indeed, the whole cosmos have their center. He is the One who came, who continues to come, and will never cease coming. The One who is present in the Eucharist is specifically the One in whom the final fulfillment is already fully anticipated.

Among many other consequences of the fulfillment of this promise, two are outstanding. We proclaim Christ's death in the light of resurrection and final glory; therefore, we can face our mortality with conviction and the hour of our death with calmness. Living on the level of the Eucharist, we will never repress the thought of our mortality; the prospect of our death does not torment us. And the other consequence is that we cannot proclaim his death and think about the death of his disciples without seeing and facing death in the light of ultimate fulfillment, in the light of that mysterious reality which we witness in the Eucharist. There can be no gap between *anamnesis*, the remembrance of the saving deed of the past, and *prolepsis*, anticipation and expectation of the final coming of Christ, of the new heaven and the new earth.

Clearly, both the eucharistic celebration and the lives of Christians marked by veneration of the Eucharist allow us to pray with great confidence, yearning, and joy: "Come, Lord Jesus!" (Rev 22:20).

In the Eucharist, we celebrate past and future in the heart of *presence:* Jesus' presence and his way of making present his and our future. The Father sends the Son who fulfills his mission of glory. Facing the horrifying moment when he, the Lamb of God, will have to make himself an offering for our sins by his nonviolent, liberating response to human violence, Jesus prays: "Now my soul is troubled. And what should I say—'Father, save me from this hour'? No, it is for this reason that I have come to this hour. Father, glorify your name." Then a voice came from heaven, 'I have glorified it, and I will glorify it again'" (Jn 12:27–28).

And for him the very glorification of the Lamb enthroned in heaven is his eucharistic mission, signifying his desire for us through and in the proclamation of his death, Resurrection, and Ascension into heaven. As in the heavenly liturgy of the Lamb, so in the Eucharist, the celebration of the Paschal Mystery reminds us of the final coming of the Lord and the final fulfillment of redemption and glorification.

For Jesus, death and resurrection are the final homecoming to the Father. The Eucharist is a sacramental assurance for Christ's disciples that he has prepared for them an eternal home in the glory of the Father. This vision in no way compromises our earthly mission. Rather, it provides us with a powerful dynamic for our mission—so that we can make "the most of the time" (Eph 5:15).

The author of the Letter to the Hebrews points all this out in a powerful way. "It is by God's will that we have been sanctified through the offering of the body of Jesus Christ once for all….Christ had offered for all time a single sacrifice for sins, 'he sat down at the right hand of God.'…For by a single offering he has perfected for all time those who are sanctified….Therefore, my friends, since we have confidence to enter the sanctuary by the blood of Jesus, by the new and living way that he opened for us through the curtain (that is, through his flesh)….Let us approach with a true heart in full assurance of faith" (Heb 10:10–22). "Let us therefore approach the throne of grace with boldness, so that we may receive mercy and find grace to help in time of need" (Heb 4:16).

"Adorers in Spirit and in Truth"

One of the awe-inspiring facts in Jesus' life was that he chose to disclose to a Samaritan woman—a person despised on several grounds—a major dimension of his mission. "The hour is coming, and is now here, when the true worshipers will worship the Father in spirit and truth, for the Father seeks such as these to worship him" (Jn 4:23–24).

In Jesus, the Father's design is fulfilled. He stands forever before the throne of the Father in his Paschal reality, offering himself in his saving, self-giving love. Forever he is the acceptable sacrifice. Through him, in the name of all humanity and of all creation, the Father receives adoration "in spirit and in truth."

It is Jesus' eucharistic mission—his whole mission—to bring the redeemed into the realm of adoration in spirit and truth. His mission is completed in his Paschal Mystery and in his everlasting presence before the throne of our gracious God. Through our adoration in spirit and truth he makes us partners in his saving love and his work of redemption. In the Eucharist, he urges us from within (living in us and with us) to unite ourselves with him, in adoration—the same kind of adoration which the Father is offered eternally by the Lamb standing before his throne.

When we celebrate the Eucharist devoutly, we let the Holy Spirit consecrate us to the loving will of God. And on our part, we dedicate ourselves—our memory, heart, mind, intelligence, and will—to him, who so graciously gives his body and blood, his whole self as gift to us. This is the spirit of adoration that marks eucharistic worship.

THREE

Fostering Eucharistic Devotions

We preserve the soundness of our faith by making care-ful distinctions between the abiding truth of revela-tion and the time-honored expression of that truth. And we do this in the community of faith under the guidance of the teaching authority of the Church.

It is impossible always and everywhere to preserve the customs and traditions of our faith without some kind of adaptation. We have to live our traditional faith in the present moment of history, and try our best to transmit it to our contemporaries in vigorous and assertive terms.

Cultures, societies, communities, economies, and politics change in accord with people's way of thinking and acting. And, as members of today's Church, we share the gifts of the

Father, Son, and Holy Spirit with the same faithful commitment as our ancestors did, although in slightly different forms that may be necessitated by new conditions.

Having reviewed a brief history of eucharistic devotion and the main dimensions of the eucharistic memorial, we now turn to the ways in which we can foster eucharistic devotion in our present day. Our purpose is to reawaken true eucharistic piety in today's world.

All the sacraments of the New Covenant open up new horizons of grace, each one demanding proper preparation and reflective acceptance of its specific grace and direction. But there is a need to cultivate a specific spirituality relating to our Lord's permanent presence in the Eucharist. It is impossible to ignore his gracious call to "be what you see and receive what you are called for! Let Christ live in your heart, mind, will, and life!"

The core of eucharistic piety is frequent remembrance of past, present, and future celebrations of the Mass: its meaning for our lives, for our concerns, endeavors, and relationships. We express this devotion in an ideal way when—before Mass—we prepare our minds and hearts for the event and—after Mass—we reflect on how, during the day or the week, we can express and foster the abiding gratitude which this eucharistic memorial evokes.

Those who attend Sunday Mass and then during the ensuing week forget what they have celebrated and received are acting irrationally. The main purpose of our eucharistic worship is to establish an ever better alliance between receiving and giving, contemplation and action, divine rites and human rights, reverence for the mystery of holiness and familiarity with Jesus, the God-Man. Only in this way will we overcome the gap between religion and daily life.

The document *Instruction on the Eucharistic Worship* (is-sued the Holy See in 1967) and the apostolic letter of John Paul II (issued in 1980) *On the Mystery and the Worship of the Eucharist* encourage the following forms of eucharistic piety: celebration of the feast of Corpus Christi and its sol-emn procession, eucharistic congresses, shorter or longer periods of exposition of the Blessed Sacrament with solemn Benediction, annual celebration of forty hours of adoration, other hours of adoration, perpetual adoration in dioceses, and, last but not least, silent prayer before the tabernacle.

In all these devotional ways of fostering a eucharistic spirit-uality, we never lose sight of the center and summit of Chris-tian life: the celebration of the eucharistic memorial (the Mass) with the reception of Holy Communion.

Corpus Christi

Around 1209, a group of holy women in Liège, Belgium, established a center dedicated to eucharistic piety. These women were convinced that the Lord desired a new feast—that of Corpus Christi—dedicated to the reserved Sacrament of the Altar. For this feast, Thomas Aquinas composed beau-tiful hymns that expertly combined dogma with devotion.

With its rich eucharistic liturgy and procession, the feast of Corpus Christi is an occasion of special praise and thanks-giving offered to the Father in the name of all creation, and of special thanksgiving for the institution of the Eucharist in which Christ's body is the bread of life. It is an extension of the praise expressed in its very institution: "On the night he was betrayed, he took bread and gave you thanks and praise....When supper was ended, he took the cup. Again he gave you thanks and praise."

Saint Augustine taught that eternal life is essentially praise and thanksgiving and that, therefore, a life lived in grateful praise is really the road to final fulfillment. The feast of Corpus Christi was and is, in many parts of the Catholic Church, an occasion for creative forms of praise and thanksgiving.

The Corpus Christi procession is a solemn act of public adoration and praise; it is in perfect harmony with the eucharistic memorial. In Catholic towns, all the houses are decorated for this procession. There is an abundance of flowers everywhere, especially before the four altars where the gospels are sung and solemn Benediction is given. And amid these beautiful artistic arrangements of flowers, church choirs and music makers of all kinds perform at their best. Members of various associations, wearing their distinctive garb, add vivid color to the occasion. All this activity points to praise of the Creator. And it is all done freely and generously. The Corpus Christi procession is a kind of cosmic liturgy. Symbolically, it invites all creatures to join in the Church's joy, gratitude, and praise. Thus, festivity and solemnity combine to mark this eucharistic celebration and procession.

Solemn Benediction is also a feature of the procession. At each altar, after the singing of the Gospel and special prayers calling for the Lord's blessing on the four corners of the earth, there is a solemn blessing with the Blessed Sacrament in the monstrance. The prayer of praise and thanksgiving is, itself, a blessing coming from God, opening our hearts for renewed graces. Ordinarily, when we bless others on various occasions, we invoke almighty God. At the solemn eucharistic Benediction, it is more evident that Christ himself blesses us and intends to make all of us a blessing for one another. And this we are, if all our life is marked by a spirit of joyous faith and praise.

Church processions, but particularly the Corpus Christi procession, symbolize among other things our pilgrimage on the road to our final destination with Christ accompanying us; for he is the Way and at the same time our final Home.

The feast of Corpus Christi, with its solemn procession, was most popular in times and areas where all were Catholics, grateful for the gift of faith and, particularly, for their faith in the Eucharist. Thanks be to God, there are still places where this is the case even today.

Eucharistic Congresses

Eucharistic congresses on the national and international levels may be compared to celebrations of the feast of Corpus Christi on an enlarged scale. Drawing large crowds, they serve as powerful inspiration for the restoration of eucharistic veneration and—especially during the last decades—for the renewal of all who participate. The latest national and international congresses have exemplified how traditional forms of eucharistic devotion can be easily adapted to new times—and this without any detriment to its former popular appeal. And, although the first eucharistic congresses met vehement opposition from Protestant churches, the more recent congresses attracted an ecumenical audience due, in part, to an increased openness among all Christians.

A eucharistic congress is an organized public assembly designed to manifest faith in the Holy Eucharist and often unified by a central theme. Participants include clergy, religious, and lay persons from many countries, as well as representatives of national and international Catholic organizations. It consists of meetings and different kinds of instruction to discuss aspects of eucharistic doctrine and practice; and also includes liturgical services and other kinds of public ceremonies.

The origins of eucharistic congresses are found in the efforts of a Frenchwoman, Marie Marthe Emilia Tamisier (1834–1910) who in the beginning directed her efforts toward encouraging people to visit places where eucharistic miracles had occurred. The first international eucharistic congress took place in 1881 at Lille in France with the blessing of Pope Leo XIII. Since then, there have been forty-six international congresses, the last two in Poland (1997) and Rome (2000).

International eucharistic congresses are supervised by the Pontifical Committee for International Eucharistic Congresses, while national and local authorities sponsor eucharistic congresses on smaller level.

Eucharistic Exposition and Benediction

The rubric of elevating the Host after the consecration and the custom of eucharistic processions arose because of the people's desire to see the consecrated Host. They were inspired with awe at the self-effacing humility of the Lord of glory, and they were filled with joy at the sight of this sacramental sign of his abiding presence. Thus began a rich development of various forms of public adoration. One of these popular forms of worship which developed in the Middle Ages is often called "Benediction of the Blessed Sacrament." After Vatican II, the Church revised its rite for the service of Benediction during which those present direct their full attention to the sight of a consecrated Host from a previous Mass in order to acknowledge the Real Presence of the risen Christ in that Host. The purpose of Benediction is to further the appreciation of the faithful for the eucharistic mystery and to increase their desire to participate fully in the Mass in which the Eucharist is consumed and shared.

Benediction consists of four parts:

1. *Exposition* in which the presider approaches the tabernacle and removes the Host, placing it in a monstrance which usually sits on the altar. The presider then uses incense to offer reverence to the Blessed Sacrament.
2. *Adoration* of the exposed Blessed Sacrament during which prayers, Scripture readings, a homily, and silence may fill the time.
3. *Benediction* in which the presider blesses the assembly with the monstrance and says a concluding prayer.
4. *Reposition*, the final part of the rite, during which the presider removes the Blessed Sacrament from the monstrance and places it back in the tabernacle. A prayer made up of acclamations called "The Divine Praises" usually concluded the Benediction, but that is not a requirement in the revised rite.

In addition to "The Divine Praises," Catholics have traditionally sung two familiar hymns during Benediction: "*O Salutaris Hostia*" and "*Pange Lingua.*" Actually, however, any suitable eucharistic hymn may be sung.

Forty Hours Devotion

In the fourteenth century, the exposition of the Blessed Sacrament in the monstrance was a popular evening devotion. Then came what is called the Forty Hours Devotion, in which our Lord's presence in the Eucharist is honored, sermons on the Blessed Sacrament are preached, and solemn sacramental Benediction is given. In Germany during this period, the devotion was so popular that the exposition of the Blessed Sacrament was held during the whole year, either in specific churches or chapels or so scheduled that there was always this special service, this uninterrupted "great prayer," in one of the churches of a diocese. Papal delegates repeatedly imposed restrictions, but the movement was very persistent. It came from the hearts of the people and was implemented by zealous priests. After the Council of Trent, the solemn exposition of the Host in the monstrance, which had previously been restricted in most countries to the feast of Corpus Christi, was promoted everywhere.

These forty hours of prayer was an ancient tradition in the whole Church, in remembrance of Jesus' forty days in the desert. And from the sixteenth century on, the forty hours of prayer before the Blessed Sacrament exposed in the monstrance became even more popular. In 1539, Paul III favored the practice by granting a special indulgence. Saint Charles Borromeo confirmed the practice for Milan in the Synod of 1565 and extended it to the whole province of Milan in 1575. Urban VIII then extended this solemn adoration to the whole Western Church. It surely served as inspiration for many Christians and Christian communities and an annual renewal of the community.

These forms of eucharistic devotion not only affirm our faith in the Real Presence of Christ in the Blessed Sacrament; they educate us in the practice of adoration, praise, and thanksgiving.

Adoration of our Lord's humble presence is an antidote to atheism and secularism, and a civilization with an unbalanced emphasis on human achievement. While it has the power to heal the withdrawal of those lost in the "lonely crowd," it does not divert us from our responsibilities in and for the world. If, in adoration we learn to let God be God in all our concerns, we shall also be able to let the world be world without allowing it to corrupt us in any way.

Holy Hour of Adoration

This eucharistic devotion consists of an hour of prayer in front of the exposed Blessed Sacrament. As a practice, the custom of the Holy Hour draws its inspiration from Christ's admonition to the apostles in Gethsemane: "Can you not watch one hour with me?"

The devotion of the Holy Hour was taught to Saint Margaret Mary Alocoque when Our Lord spoke these words to her sometime in June 1674: "Every week between Thursday and Friday I will grant you a share in that mortal sadness which I chose to feel in the Garden of Olives. You shall keep me company in the prayer I then offered to my Father." This devotion is also seen as one of the special practices associated with devotion to the Sacred Heart.

Later in the nineteenth century, a French Jesuit founded a confraternity known as the Archconfraternity of the Holy Hour to help spread this devotion. From France, this devotion spread to many other countries.

Perpetual Adoration of the Eucharist

Perpetual Adoration is a eucharistic devotion in which people of a particular church or diocese or religious community practice uninterrupted adoration of the Blessed Sacrament during the day and night for seven days a week without end. In some cases, Perpetual Adoration takes place in a small yet secure chapel apart from the main church building.

From a practical standpoint, the concept of Perpetual Adoration developed out of the devotion of Forty Hours, begun in 1534. In 1642 Baron de Renty, who was famous for his devotion to the Blessed Sacrament, founded an association of women in Paris for what was practically perpetual adoration. A few years later, in 1654, a Benedictine named Mechtilde founded the first community of Benedictines of the Perpetual Adoration of the Blessed Sacrament. Since then, many religious communities have made eucharistic adoration either the main or an essential part of their rule of life.

One of the most famous, perhaps, is the Society of the Most Blessed Sacrament, founded in 1857 by Saint Peter Julian Eymard. There are several classes of members, one being the contemplative who are consecrated to perpetual adoration, another being the religious who promote devotion to the Eucharist, and one being a lay or Third Order group who follow only part of the rule.

The Congregation for the Sacraments and Divine Worship has ruled that perpetual adoration of the Blessed Sacrament in parishes is allowed by the church; however, the local bishop has the final say concerning its practice in his diocese. Pope John Paul II is an advocate of eucharistic adoration. He started daily adoration with exposition of the Blessed Sacrament in St. Peter's Basilica; and he erected a perpetual adoration chapel in Rome at the prompting of Mother Teresa.

Reverence for the Viaticum

Through the centuries, the main reason for reservation of the Blessed Sacrament has been prompted by the need for the Viaticum for the dying. In the beginning, the Blessed Sacrament was brought to the sick and the dying by the priest immediately after the eucharistic celebration. This was done to preserve the connection between the Mass and our Lord's Divine Presence which is a direct result of the eucharistic celebration. But this method changed through the years. At one period, the Blessed Sacrament was brought either by members of the sick person's family or by a deacon. Also, there were times when family members were allowed to care for its reservation so that the sick person could receive Communion explicitly as Viaticum as soon as he or she felt death approaching. It has always been a matter of great concern to the Church that the sick have access to the Viaticum and to frequent Communion during long-lasting illness.

As early as the thirteenth century, the faithful, carrying candles in their hands, were invited to accompany the Blessed Sacrament from the church to the house of the sick person, in a kind of eucharistic procession. In those days, people were always happy to do this. In rural Catholic communities where more leisure time was available for devotional practices, this custom caused no problems. The faithful would appear at least at the doorways of their houses to receive the sacramental blessing.

However times may change, the wonderful fact that Jesus remains in the Blessed Sacrament, ever ready to console the sick, should enkindle special devotion, gratitude, and adoration. It also should be and, indeed, is for many believers a strong motive to share in Jesus' love for the sick and dying.

If possible, the whole family should gather and welcome the Lord when the Blessed Sacrament is brought to the sick in the home. Great care should be taken that sick persons are given the opportunity to receive Holy Communion frequently, and especially that those in danger of death receive the Viaticum while still fully conscious.

In view of the shortage of priests and deacons, qualified people—often senior citizens—can render valuable services in caring for the lonely and sick by loving care and prayerful assistance. In many Catholic parishes these good people are entrusted with this special ministry: They bring the Blessed Sacrament to the sick for whom they also care in other ways. And, at the proper time, they inform the pastor when those under their care should receive the anointing of the sick. At that time they not only prepare the room with table, cross, and candles, but they also patiently pray with words of faith and comfort for fruitful reception of the sacraments. It would be good for us to practice some of these old traditions.

Private Visits to the Blessed Sacrament

Time spent reflecting in the presence of Jesus Christ is time gratefully accepted from the Lord of history, who graces us here on earth with his loving presence. It is time that merits for us eternal life.

People who think they are too busy should listen to the call, "Sleeper, awake! / Rise from the dead, / and Christ will shine on you" (Eph 5:14). If we become thankfully aware of Christ's presence, he—the one who is light of the world and wants to make us, in him and with him, light for the world—alerts our senses to a fuller life, to the true light. From this short exposure to Christ in our visits to the Blessed Sacrament, there arises also a sharper awareness of the preciousness of time: "Make the most of the time, because the days are evil" (Eph 5:16).

A priest once asked a young man, whom he saw spending hours before the tabernacle: "What do you do all this time?" The response was simple: "I let my soul enjoy the sunshine!"

To better utilize this time in God's presence it might be well to pursue the following objectives.

Adore God

The burning lamp near the tabernacle says to us: Remember the gracious nearness of Jesus who came like a candle to bring warmth, peace, and light into the world, and spent himself finally on the cross to enter into the fullness of the Father's glory.

Before the tabernacle we adore the eternal Word who took flesh, became one of us to enlighten everyone. In adoration of the mystery of God's condescendence, our faith in the Paschal Mystery lifts our hearts, and we meditate on the word of the Seer of Patmos: "At once I was in the spirit, and there in heaven stood a throne, with one seated on the throne. And the one seated there looks like jasper and carnelian, and around the throne is a rainbow that looks like an emerald. ...Then I saw between the throne and the four living creatures and among the elders a Lamb standing as if it had been slaughtered" (Rev 4:2; 5:6). Turning our eyes and hearts to this Lamb, we say with Thomas: "My Lord and my God!"

The Lamb standing before the Father's throne is the eternal intercessor. The Father remembers forever that his Son-made-Man bears this slaughter for us, thus calling to mind his "holy covenant" (Lk 1:72).

Silent adoration before the tabernacle is a wholesome remembrance, a kind of training for a healthy, grateful memory that brings us closer to the Faithful One who remembers us by his gracious presence in our midst.

To make more fruitful our time of remembrance before the tabernacle or monstrance, here are two suggestions. One is to meditate from time to time on the official eucharistic prayers of the Mass, word by word. By letting the words enter deeply into our hearts, we will experience the depth and wealth of these texts with greater joy during our next participation in the Mass.

The other suggestion is that, in the presence of Jesus who stands before the Father as the Lamb marked by the signs of slaughter, we meditate on all the great mysteries of creation: the Incarnation of the Word of God, the Passion, death, Resurrection, and Ascension into heaven of Jesus, and the descent of the Holy Spirit on his Church. Then, thus reminded, we examine our own life history and lead it, point by point, into thanksgiving for the countless blessings we have received. We don't leave out our disappointments, our sufferings, or our daily crosses; we try to fit them into the whole picture as they blend with the Lamb marked by the signs of slaughter. We then praise the Lord who, through his death, his Resurrection, and his eucharistic union with us, has given our wounds a new meaning for ourselves and for others.

As we sit or kneel before the tabernacle, we should be ever thankful that so many happenings, which for unbelievers prove to be sheer frustration, make sense for believers who begin to share in the history of salvation because they are living in profound union with the Holy Redeemer.

"Lord, Here I Am!"

Before the self-giving presence of Jesus in the Blessed Sacrament we remember the many times when he nourished our faith, hope, and love with his body and his blood. By giving himself to us, he encourages us to give ourselves to him. Our reflective adoration before the Sacrament of Abiding Presence becomes a prayer of readiness *now:* "Lord, here I am! Accept me! Transform me! Send me!" And we begin to examine the critical areas of our daily life: our relationships with our neighbors, with those who misunderstand us, with those who oppose us, with those who need greater love and affirmation from us, and with those who need our healing and reconciling love.

In his letter *On the Mystery and Worship of the Eucharist,* John Paul II writes: "This veneration [of the Eucharist] arises from love and fosters the love to which we are called." Let us, then, constantly pray to "the Lamb marked with the signs of slaughter" for the same kind of love that he has shown us. He died for us sinners, offered himself up for us who, by our sins, have rebelled against him. On the Cross he cried out to the Father for us, "Father, forgive! They do not realize what they are doing."

By creating a new life within us at Holy Communion, he calls us to imitate his kind of love. In this light, we take a new look at our relationships with those who have hurt us or those whom we have hurt. We pray to Jesus to conform our hearts to his, to strengthen us with a healing, reconciling love. Should we not also pray frequently before the tabernacle: "Lord, heal us, for we have sinned against you," and thus open ourselves to the charism of healing love that will wipe out all hatred?

And as we bring our personal experiences, our individual needs, and all our hurts to Jesus in the Blessed Sacrament, we cannot forget that the object of our adoration is the "Lamb of God who takes upon himself the burden of the sin of the world," the Peacemaker who prevails over violence. In his presence, our prayer, "Lord, here I am!" becomes mission and readiness to make our best contribution for a peaceful world, a system of nonviolence everywhere and on all levels.

Try to Understand God's Will for You

We spend our time well before the tabernacle in silent prayer, meditation, and thanksgiving when, under the eyes of Jesus, the Lamb marked with the signs of slaughter, we try to discern what the will of God is for us. We know that we can do nothing for salvation by ourselves. Therefore, we should listen to the exhortation of the apostle: "Be filled with the Spirit" (Eph 5:18).

When we gratefully allow Jesus to "shine upon us" and illumine us by the mysteries on which we meditate and which we glorify in this sacrament, we can be assured that the Holy Spirit will permeate us, guide us, and strengthen us. Our willing attitude puts us on the same wavelength as the Holy Spirit, who will help us to examine our desires, refine our plans, and analyze our capabilities so that we can sincerely offer them to Jesus as signs of our ardent gratitude. It is then that we begin to see clearly what we have to renounce and what we have to cultivate in ourselves and in our surroundings and lifestyles.

Pray, "Come, Lord Jesus!"

We have seen that the sacramental presence of Jesus in the Eucharist is the Paschal Mystery reaching out to us. It is the

Paschal Mystery made present by the coming of Jesus, who is the glory of the Father. Our eucharistic veneration would be neither sound nor healing if we were to neglect this dimension. We look forward to the final coming of the Lord. "The Spirit and the bride say, 'Come.' / And let everyone who hears say, 'Come.' / And let everyone who is thirsty come. / Let anyone who wishes take the water of life as a gift" (Rev 22:17).

A genuine eucharistic devotion causes us to long for the final coming of the Lord, to long for our homecoming and for the homing of all creation into the ultimate freedom of the children of our Father. God is infinitely generous and rich in his gifts. But the gift of freedom will be given only to those who desire it. Eucharistic worship helps us to free ourselves from useless desires and cares, and opens us to the living water that wells up for eternal life.

Our willingness to pray, "Lord, here I am!" and our effort to discern, in the presence of the Lord, what the will of God is, prepare us for our mission, our responsibility in the world. The more we listen to him who promises, "Surely I am coming soon," the more our manner of life responds: "Amen, come, Lord Jesus!" (Rev 22:20).

Submit to Him With the Words:
"Your Kingdom Come"

Although we emphasize the importance of eucharistic devotion here, we do so with no intention of "privatizing" religion. When we say with the Spirit, "Come!" we also pray with all our heart, "Your kingdom come." Through eucharistic veneration, we even enter more deeply into the dimensions of the kingdom of God, a kingdom of love, peace, and justice.

In silent contemplation and adoration before the Blessed Sacrament, before the Lamb with the marks of slaughter upon him, we open ourselves to his liberating love, his saving justice, his forgiving mission. We speak to our Lord, "Here I am, send me!" And with a heart earnestly craving that the kingdom of God may reach all people, we pray that God's will be done. Letting our devotion shine before the world, we can hope that our actions will turn people's attention to the Lord when they see the good we do (see Mt 5:16).

FOUR

Eucharistic Prayers and Devotions

Formats for a Visit to the Blessed Sacrament

The following three formats, each different, are offered here as models for prayer in the presence of the Blessed Sacrament. They are meant as guidance only and should be tailored to the needs of the individual, the season of the liturgical year, and the time available.

Format One

Prayer of Preparation

O Lord, give me the words to adequately praise your holy presence in the eucharistic sacrament. Remove from me the spirit of pride and resistance to your will for me. Cleanse me of every sin of body and spirit. Purify my heart of all distractions, worldly concerns, and sinful thoughts. Give me also the grace to understand and the will to proceed worthily so that I may pray to you with attentive devotion before your eternal Majesty. We pray this through our Lord Jesus Christ, your son, who lives and reigns with you and the Holy Spirit, for ever and ever. Amen.

Hail Mary...
Our Father...

Hymn

Sing, my tongue, the Savior's glory,
Of his flesh the myst'ry sing:
Of the blood, all price exceeding,
Shed by our immortal King,
Destined for the world's redemption,
From a noble womb to spring.

Of a pure and spotless virgin
Born for us on earth below,
He, as man with man conversing,
Stayed the seeds of truth to sow;
Then he closed in solemn order
Wondrously his life of woe.

On the night of that last supper
Seated with his chosen band,
He, the paschal victim eating,
First fulfills the law's command;
Then as food to his apostles
Gives himself with his own hand.

Word made flesh, the bread of nature
By his word to flesh he turns;
Wine into his blood he changes:
What through sense no change discerns?
Only be the heart in earnest,
Faith her lesson quickly learns.

To the everlasting Father,
And the Son who reigns on high
With the Holy Ghost proceeding
Forth from each eternally,
Be salvation, honor, blessing,
Might and endless majesty.

> SAINT THOMAS AQUINAS
> *PANGE LINGUA GLORIOSI*
> TRANSLATED BY EDWARD CASWALL, 1814–1878

Prayer

Come let us praise the Lord with joyful hearts. Let us sing joyfully to God our Savior. Let us pray in his presence with thankfulness and let us make joyful noise to him with all our being. Amen.

Psalm 147 (146)

How good it is to sing to our God,
how sweet and befitting to praise him!
The Lord rebuilds Jerusalem;
he gathers the exiles of Israel;
he heals their broken hearts
and binds up their wounds.

He determines the number of stars,
he calls each of them by name.
The Lord is great and mighty in power;
his wisdom in beyond measure.
The Lord lifts up the humble,
but casts the wicked to the ground.

Sing to the Lord with thanksgiving,
make music on the harp for our God.
With clouds he covers the sky,
and provides the earth with rain;
he covers the hills with grass,
and with plants for man to cultivate.

He provides food for the cattle,
even for the young ravens when they call.
He is not concerned with the strength of a horse;
nor is he pleased with men's bravery;
The Lord delights in those who fear him
and expect him to care for them.

Exalt the Lord, O Jerusalem;
praise your God, O Zion!
For he strengthens the bars of your gates
and blesses your children within you.

He grants peace on your borders
and feeds you with the finest grain.

He sends his command to the earth
and swiftly runs his word.
He spreads snow like wool;
he scatters frost like ashes.
He hurls down hail like pebbles;
who will stand before his icy blasts?

But he sends his word and melts the snow;
he makes his breeze blow,
and again the waters flow.

It is he who tells Jacob his words,
his laws and decrees to Israel.
This he has not done for other nations,
so his laws remain unknown to them.

CHRISTIAN COMMUNITY BIBLE

First Eucharistic Scripture Reading

To continue with my advice, I cannot praise you, for your gatherings are not for the better but for the worse.

First, as I have heard, when you gather together, there are divisions among you and I partly believe it. There may have to be different groups among you, so that it plainly appears who are approved among you.

Your gatherings are no longer the Supper of the Lord, for each one eats at once his own food and while one is hungry, the other is getting drunk. Do you not have houses in which to eat and drink? Or perhaps you despise the Church of God and desire to humiliate those who have nothing? What shall I say? Shall I praise you? For this I cannot praise you.

This is the tradition of the Lord that I received and then in my turn I have handed on to you; the Lord Jesus, on the night that he was delivered up, took bread and, after giving thanks, broke it, saying, "This is my body which is broken for you; do this in memory of me." In the same manner, taking the cup after supper, he said, "This cup is the new Covenant in my blood. Whenever you drink it, do it in memory of me." So, then, whenever you eat of this bread and drink from this cup, you are proclaiming the death of the Lord until he comes.

Therefore, if anyone eats of the bread or drinks from the cup of the Lord unworthily, he sins against the body and blood of the Lord.

1 CORINTHIANS 11:17–27 (CCB)

Prayer

O Father, giver of your Son and of every good thing.
Give us bread for our physical well-being,
and give us the nourishment of your word
and of your doctrine for our spiritual strength.
Through Christ, Our Lord. Amen.

Second Eucharistic Scripture Reading

"I am the bread of life. Though your ancestors ate the manna in the desert, they died. But here you have the *bread which comes from heaven* so that you may eat of it and not die.

"I am the living *bread which has come from heaven*; whoever eats of this bread will live forever. The bread I shall give is my flesh and I will give it for the life of the world."

The Jews were arguing among themselves, "How can this man give us (his) flesh to eat?" So Jesus replied, "Truly, I say to you, if you do not eat the flesh of the Son of Man and drink his blood, you have no life in you. He who eats my flesh and drinks my blood lives with eternal life and I will raise him up on the last day."

JOHN 6:48–54 (CCB)

Prayer

United with Christ in the bond of the Eucharist, we keep watch here in faithful love of you, Our Father. We have come to offer adoration to your Son who lays down his human life for us and our salvation. May our prayers lead us to the light of eternal life, even as the star led the Magi to your infant Son in the stable. We ask this through Christ our Lord. Amen.

Eucharistic Meditation

Do you realize that Jesus is there in the tabernacle expressly for you—for you alone? He burns with the desire to come into your heart....Don't listen to the demon, laugh at him, and go without fear to receive the Jesus of peace and love....

Receive Communion often, very often....There you have the sole remedy, if you want to be cured. Jesus has not put this attraction into your heart for nothing....

The guest of our soul knows our misery; He comes to find an empty tent within us—that is all He asks.

SAINT THÉRÈSE OF LISIEUX

Prayers of Intercession

To the Lord of all life we pray:

> You graciously give to your people the bread of life,
> We ask that you bring us out of the death caused by sin.

As we eat this bread and drink this cup,
we proclaim your death and Resurrection, Lord Jesus.

You give us hope from the supper your Son gave to us in this world.
May we find contentment in this meal that we share.

As we eat this bread and drink this cup,
we proclaim your death and Resurrection, Lord Jesus.

You give us love through the blood your Son poured out for us.
May we be washed clean of all our sins.

As we eat this bread and drink this cup,
we proclaim your death and Resurrection, Lord Jesus.

You give to the world the promise of life eternal.
We ask that you claim for your own all those who have died.

As we eat this bread and drink this cup,
we proclaim your death and Resurrection, Lord Jesus.

Litany of Praise to the Holy Name of Jesus

Lord, have mercy on us. Christ, have mercy on us.
Lord, have mercy on us. Jesus, hear us. Jesus,
    graciously hear us.
God the Father of heaven, have mercy on us.
God the Son, Redeemer of the world, have mercy on us.
God the Holy Spirit, have mercy on us.
Holy Trinity, one God, have mercy on us.

Jesus, Son of the Living God, have mercy on us.
Jesus, splendor of the Father, have mercy on us.

Jesus, brightness of eternal light, have mercy on us.

Jesus, king of glory, have mercy on us.

Jesus, Sun of Justice, have mercy on us.

Jesus, son of the Virgin Mary, have mercy on us.

Jesus, most amiable, have mercy on us.

Jesus, most admirable, have mercy on us.

Jesus, mighty God, have mercy on us.

Jesus, Father of the world to come, have mercy on us.

Jesus, angel of the great counsel, have mercy on us.

Jesus, most powerful, have mercy on us.

Jesus, most patient, have mercy on us.

Jesus, most obedient, have mercy on us.

Jesus, meek and humble of heart, have mercy on us.

Jesus, lover of chastity, have mercy on us.

Jesus, lover of us, have mercy on us.

Jesus, God of peace, have mercy on us.

Jesus, author of life, have mercy on us.

Jesus, model of all virtues, have mercy on us.

Jesus, zealous lover of souls, have mercy on us.

Jesus, our God, have mercy on us.

Jesus, our refuge, have mercy on us.

Jesus, Father of the poor, have mercy on us.

Jesus, true light, have mercy on us.

Jesus, eternal wisdom, have mercy on us.

Jesus, Good Shepherd, have mercy on us.

Jesus, true light, have mercy on us.

Jesus, eternal wisdom, have mercy on us.

Jesus, infinite goodness, have mercy on us.

Jesus, our way and our life, have mercy on us.

Jesus, joy of angels, have mercy on us.

Jesus, king of patriarchs, have mercy on us.

Jesus, master of apostles, have mercy on us.

Jesus, teacher of evangelists, have mercy on us.
Jesus, strength of martyrs, have mercy on us.
Jesus, light of confessors, have mercy on us.
Jesus, purity of virgins, have mercy on us.
Jesus, crown of all saints, have mercy on us.

Be merciful, spare us, O Jesus.
Be merciful, graciously hear us, O Jesus.
From all evil, O Jesus, deliver us.
From all sin, O Jesus, deliver us.
From your wrath, O Jesus, deliver us.
From the snares of the devil, O Jesus, deliver us.
From everlasting death, O Jesus, deliver us.
From the neglect of your inspirations, O Jesus, deliver us.
Through the mystery of your Incarnation,
    O Jesus, deliver us.
Through your nativity, O Jesus, deliver us.
Through your infancy, O Jesus, deliver us.
Through your most divine life, O Jesus, deliver us.
Through your labors, O Jesus, deliver us.
Through your agony and passion, O Jesus, deliver us.
Through your Cross, O Jesus, deliver us.
Through your death and burial, O Jesus, deliver us.
Through your Resurrection, O Jesus, deliver us.
Through your ascension, O Jesus, deliver us.
Through your institution of the Most Holy Eucharist,
    O Jesus, deliver us.
Through your joys, O Jesus, deliver us.
Through your glory, O Jesus, deliver us.

Lamb of God, who takes away the sins of the world,
    spare us, O Jesus.

Lamb of God, who takes away the sins of the world,
    have mercy on us, O Jesus.
Jesus, hear us.
Jesus, graciously hear us. Amen.

Format Two

Prayer of Preparation

Let us witness the holiness of the most pure Body and Blood
of Our Lord and Savior Jesus Christ, who, having descended
from heaven, is distributed among us. He is the life, the hope,
the Resurrection, the cleansing, and the remission of sins.
Amen.

Sing a psalm to our immortal, heavenly King, who sits on
the chariot of the Cherubim.
Sing a psalm to the Lord, O you Choirs.
Sing to him in a sweet voice,
for the psalms, and their melodies are fitting for him.
You his ministers praise the Lord in the heavens,
for Christ is brought and distributed to us here on earth.
Alleluia.
He gives us his body for our food,
and washes us with his holy blood, Alleluia.
Come near to the Lord, and receive his light, Alleluia.
Taste and see how good the Lord is, Alleluia.
Bless the Lord in the heavens, Alleluia.
Bless him in the highest, Alleluia.
Bless him all you his angels, Alleluia.

    Armenian Liturgy

Hail Mary...
Our Father...

Hymn

Shepherd of souls, refresh and bless
Your chosen pilgrim flock
With manna in the wilderness,
With water from the rock.

Hungry and thirsty, faint and weak,
As you were here below,
Our souls the joy celestial seek
Which from your sorrows flow.

We would not live by bread alone,
But by that word of grace,
In strength of which we travel on
To our abiding place.

JAMES MONTGOMERY, 1865

Prayer

Come, O Lord Our God, from your throne of glory in your kingdom. Come and sanctify us, you who sit above with the Father but who is here invisibly present with us. Come and help us give worthy thanks to you for all the gifts which you have lavished on us. You who have given us these gifts allow us to be faithful witnesses to your real presence in the holy Eucharist and let us be united to your Body and Blood so that we may have Christ dwelling in our hearts. We pray this through our Lord Jesus Christ, your son, for ever and ever. Amen.

Psalm 81 (80)

Sing joyfully to God, our strength;
acclaim aloud the God of Jacob.
Start the music, strike the timbrel,
play melodies on the harp and lyre.
Sound the trumpet at the new moon,
on our feast day when the moon is full.
This is a decree for Israel,
an ordinance of the God of Jacob,
A statute he wrote for Joseph
when he went out of Egypt.

They heard a voice they did not know:
"Open wide your mouth and I will fill it,
I relieved your shoulder from burden;
I freed your hands.
You called in distress, and I saved you;
unseen, I answered you in thunder;
I tested you at the waters of Meribah.

Hear, my people, as I admonish you,
If only you would listen, O Israel!
There shall be no strange god among you,
you shall not worship any alien god,
for I the Lord am your God,
who led you forth from the land of Egypt.

But my people did not listen;
Israel did not obey.
So I gave them over to their stubbornness
and they followed their own counsels.

If only my people would listen,
if only Israel would walk in my ways,
I would quickly subdue their adversaries
and turn my hand against their enemies.
Those who hate the Lord would cringe before him,
and their panic would last forever.
I would feed you with the finest wheat
and satisfy you with honey from the rock."

First Eucharistic Scripture Reading

But now Christ has appeared as the high priest with regard to the good things of these new times. He passed through a sanctuary more noble and perfect, not made by hands, that is, not created. He did not take with himself the blood of goats and bulls but his own blood, when he entered once and for all into this sanctuary after obtaining definitive redemption. If the sprinkling of people defiled by sin with the blood of goats and bulls or with the ashes of a heifer provides them with exterior cleanness and holiness, how much more will it be with the blood of Christ? He, moved by the eternal Spirit, offered himself as an unblemished victim to God and his blood cleanses us from dead works, so that we may serve the living God.

So Christ is the mediator of a new covenant or testament. His death made atonement for the sins committed under the old testament, and the promise is handed over to all who are called to the everlasting inheritance. With every testament it is necessary to wait until its author has died. For a testament infers death and has no value while the maker of it is still alive.

That is why the first covenant was not ratified without blood. Moses proclaimed to the assembled people all the commandments of the Law; then he took the blood of bulls and goats and mixed it with water, hyssop and red wool, and sprinkled the book of the Covenant and the people saying: *This is the blood of the Covenant that God commanded you.* In the same way he sprinkled with blood the Sanctuary and all the objects of the ritual. According to the Law, almost all cleansings have to be performed with blood; there is no forgiveness without the shedding of blood.

HEBREWS 9:11–22 (CCB)

Prayer

Lord God, you who have sent your Son to establish the new and perfect covenant which binds us intimately to you, grant that the blood of Christ may be an everlasting source of life for us. May we always acknowledge this source of life through which we have been redeemed; may this blood be sign of faith in your promises. Through Christ, Our Lord. Amen.

Second Eucharistic Scripture Reading

They were faithful to the teaching of the apostles, the common life of sharing, the breaking of bread and the prayers.

A holy fear came upon all the people, for many wonders and miraculous signs were done by the apostles. Now all the believers lived together and shared all their belongings. They would sell their property and all they had and distribute the proceeds to others according to their need. Each day they met together in the Temple area; they broke bread in their homes; they shared their food with great joy and simplicity of heart; they praised God and won the people's favor. And every day the Lord added to their number those who were being saved.

ACTS 2:42–47 (CCB)

Prayer

Make us truly a eucharistic community, Lord, aware of the source that gives life to each of us and trustful of the certainty of your eternal love. Let us stretch out our hands to each other and to all those in need of your hope, your help, and your healing. Through Christ Our Lord. Amen.

Eucharistic Meditation

"Rabbi, where are you staying?" Each day the Church responds: Christ is present in the Eucharist, in the sacrament of his death and Resurrection. In and through the Eucharist, you acknowledge the dwelling-place of the Living God in human history. For the Eucharist is the Sacrament of the Love which conquers death. It is the Sacrament of the Covenant, pure Gift of Love for the reconciliation of all humanity. It is the gift of the Real Presence of Jesus the Redeemer, in the bread which is His Body given up for us, in the wine which is His Blood poured out for all. Thanks to the Eucharist, constantly renewed among all peoples of the world, Christ continues to build his church: He brings us together in praise and thanksgiving for salvation, in the communion which only infinite love can forge....Dear friends, may your presence here mean a true commitment in faith. For Christ is now answering your own question and the questions of all those who seek the Living God. He answers by offering an invitation: This is my Body, take it and eat. To the Father, He entrusts his supreme desire: that all those whom He loves may be one in the same communion.

POPE JOHN PAUL II
WORLD YOUTH DAY HOMILY, AUGUST 24, 1997

Prayers of Intercession

To the Lord of all life we pray:

Help us to be a community of peace, for if we are not peaceful ourselves, we cannot create peace in others.

Send us your light, your peace, and your presence that conquers all hatred and anger.

Help us to renew our efforts to be peaceful to all whom we meet during the day, for you can bring order and love to the most ordinary of circumstances.

Send us your light, your peace, and your presence that conquers all hatred and anger.

Help us to participate in true peace, not in cease fires, not in armed truces, nor in silent and resentful tolerance, for only you, the Prince of Peace, can bring us peace that passes all understanding.

Send us your light, your peace, and your presence that conquers all hatred and anger.

Offer us your assurances that those who have gone before us will find peace everlasting with you in heaven.

Send us your light, your peace, and your presence as we travel on our own salvation journey and eventually rejoice with you and the communion of saints in the perfect peace of your heavenly home.

Litany of Praise
for the Blessed Sacrament

Lord, have mercy on us. *Christ, have mercy on us.*
Lord, have mercy on us. Christ, hear us.
Christ graciously hear us.
God, the Father of Heaven, *have mercy on us.*
God, the Son, Redeemer of the world, *have mercy on us.*
Holy Trinity, one God, *have mercy on us.*

Living Bread, that came down from Heaven,
have mercy on us.
Hidden God and savior, *have mercy on us.*
Wheat of the elect, *have mercy on us.*
Wine of which virgins are the fruit, *have mercy on us.*
Bread of abundance, *have mercy on us.*
Perpetual sacrifice, *have mercy on us.*
Clean oblation, *have mercy on us.*
Lamb without spot, *have mercy on us.*
Most pure feast, *have mercy on us.*
Food of angels, *have mercy on us.*
Hidden manna, *have mercy on us.*
Memorial of the wonders of God, *have mercy on us.*
Super-substantial Bread, *have mercy on us.*
Word made flesh, dwelling in us, *have mercy on us.*
Sacred Host, *have mercy on us.*
Chalice of benediction, *have mercy on us.*
Mystery of faith, *have mercy on us.*
Most holy of all sacrifices, *have mercy on us.*
Heavenly antidote against the poison of sin,
have mercy on us.
Most wonderful of all miracles, *have mercy on us.*

Holy Commemoration of the Passion of Christ,
have mercy on us.
Memorial of divine love, *have mercy on us.*
Overflowing of divine bounty, *have mercy on us.*
Medicine of immortality, *have mercy on us.*
Live-giving sacrament, *have mercy on us.*
Bread made flesh by the power of the Word,
have mercy on us.
Unbloody Sacrifice, *have mercy on us.*
At once our feast and our Guest, *have mercy on us.*
Bond of charity, *have mercy on us.*
Priest and Victim, *have mercy on us.*
Refreshment of holy souls, *have mercy on us.*
Pledge of future glory, *have mercy on us.*

Be merciful, *spare us, O Lord.*
Be merciful, *graciously hear us, O Lord.*

From an unworthy reception of your Body and Blood,
O Lord, deliver us.
From the pride of life, *O Lord, deliver us.*
From every occasion of sin, *O Lord, deliver us.*
Through the desire with which you longed to eat this
Passover with your disciples, *O Lord, deliver us.*
Through the humility with which you washed their feet,
O Lord, deliver us.
Through the love by which you instituted this Divine
Sacrament, *O Lord, deliver us.*
Through your Precious Blood, which you did leave upon
our altars, *O Lord, deliver us.*
Through the five wounds of this your most holy Body,
O Lord, deliver us.

We sinners beseech you, hear us,

That you will preserve and increase our faith, and devotion toward this Sacrament, *we beseech you, hear us.*

That you will conduct us, through true confession of our sins, to a frequent reception of the Holy Eucharist, *we beseech you, hear us.*

That you will deliver us form all unfaithfulness and blindness of heart, *we beseech you, hear us.*

That you will grant to us the heavenly fruits of this Most Holy Sacrament, *we beseech you, hear us.*

That at the hour of our death you will strengthen and defend us by this heavenly Viaticum, *we beseech you, hear us.*

Son of God, *we beseech you, hear us.*

Lamb of God, who takes away the sins of the world, *spare us, O Lord.*

Lamb of God, who takes away the sins of the world, *graciously hear us, O Lord.*

Lamb of God, who takes away the sins of the world, *have mercy on us.*

Let us pray: O God, who in this Sacrament has left us a memorial of your Passion, grant us the grace, we ask of you, so to venerate the sacred mysteries of your Body and Blood, that we may ever continue to feel within ourselves the blessed fruit of your redemption, who lives and reigns, God forever and ever. Amen.

Format Three

Prayer of Preparation

O God, who made the seas and the dry lands, the stars and the sun, let us come and adore you in your most sacred mystery of the Eucharist. Let us fall down on our knees before you and let us weep for our sins in the presence of the Lord who made us, for you are our Lord and we are your people. Amen.

> *Hail Mary...*
> *Our Father...*

Hymn

At the Lamb's high feast we sing,
Praise to our victorious King,
Who has washed us in the tide
Flowing from his pierced side;
Praise we him, whose love divine
Gives his sacred blood for wine,
Gives his body for the feast,
Christ the Victim, Christ the Priest.

Where the Paschal blood is poured,
Death's dark angel sheathes his sword;
Israel's hosts triumphant go
Through the wave that drowns the foe.
Praise we Christ, whose blood was shed,
Paschal Victim, Paschal Bread;
With sincerity and love
Eat we Manna from above.

AD REGIAS AGNI DAPES (FOURTH CENTURY)
TRANSLATED BY ROBERT CAMPELL, 1814–1868

Prayer

With confidence, we pray to the Lamb of God that this time spent in prayer in front of your eucharistic presence will be a fruitful effort. You, the Lamb of God, who protected your people from the angel of death, mark the doors of our hearts with your saving blood. Bring us and all our beloved dead to your wedding feast in heaven where all is praise and rejoicing. Amen.

Psalm 23 (22)

The Lord is my shepherd, I shall not want.
He makes me lie down in green pastures.
He leads me beside the still waters.
He restores my soul.
He guides me through the right paths
    for his name's sake.

Although I walk through the valley
of the shadow of death,
I fear no evil,
for you are beside me.
Your rod and your staff
are there to comfort me.
You spread a table before me
in the presence of my foes.
You anoint my head with oil;
my cup is overflowing.

Goodness and kindness will follow me
all the days of my life,
I shall dwell in the house of the Lord
as long as I live.

CHRISTIAN COMMUNITY BIBLE

First Eucharistic Scripture Reading

On the first day of the Festival of the Unleavened Bread, the day when the Passover Lamb was killed, the disciples asked him, "Where would you have us go to prepare the Passover meal for you?"

So Jesus sent two of his disciples with these instructions, "Go into the city and there a man will come to you carrying a jar of water. Follow him to the house he enters and say to the owner, 'The Master says: Where is the room where I may eat the Passover meal with my disciples?' Then he will show you a large room upstairs, already arranged and furnished. There you will prepare for us." The disciples went off. When they reached the city, they found everything just as Jesus had told them; and they prepared the Passover meal.

When it was evening, Jesus arrived with the Twelve....While they were eating, Jesus took bread, blessed and broke it, and gave it to them. And he said, "Take this, it is my body." Then he took a cup and after he had given thanks, passed it to them and they all drank from it. And he said, "This is my blood, the blood of the Covenant, which is to be poured out for many. Truly, I say to you, I will not taste the fruit of the vine again until the day I drink the new wine in the kingdom of God."

MARK 14:12–16, 22–26 (CCB)

Prayer

Holy Lord and Father, you gather us around the table of your Son, who was given for our salvation. Grant that we may not fall prey to the lure of earthly goods nor participate in the shortsighted quest for successes in this life, but may your Son bring us enlightenment so that we may discern the passing from the eternal, the true from the false. Through Christ our Lord. Amen.

Second Eucharistic Scripture Reading

Then they [the Jews] said, "Show us miraculous signs, that we may see and believe you. What sign do you perform? Our ancestors ate manna in the desert; as Scripture says: *They were given bread from heaven to eat.*"

Jesus then said to them, "Truly, I say to you, it was not Moses who gave you the *bread from heaven.* My Father gives you the true *bread from heaven.* The bread God gives is the One who comes from heaven and gives life to the world." And they said, "Give us this bread always."

Jesus said to them, "I am the bread of life; he who comes to me shall never be hungry, and he who believes in me shall never be thirsty."

JOHN 6:30–36 (CCB)

Prayer

Father of Mercy, whose Son Jesus multiplied the loaves and fishes for a hungry crowd, free us from making material interests a priority. Father of Mercy, whose Son left the bread and wine as a remembrance of him, grant that we who eat his body and drink his blood may be signs to all of his great promise of life and true liberation. Father of Mercy, whose Son resisted the temptation to transform stones into bread, strengthen our desire to avoid all temptation. Through Christ our Lord. Amen.

Eucharistic Meditation

Many people make pilgrimages to distant places to venerate the relics of the saints, where, hearing with wonder the report of their miracles and gazing in awe at the magnificent churches erected in their honor, they kiss these sacred bones enshrined in golden reliquaries. Yet right here with me are You, my God, present on the altar, You, the Most Holy, the Creator of all peoples and the Lord of the angels. On such pilgrimages travelers are often led by curiosity and love of novelty, and seldom do we hear that they come back with much spiritual gain. But here in the Sacrament of the altar, You, my God, are wholly present, You the fruit of eternal salvation is bestowed, as often as You are worthily and devoutly received. It is not curiosity or levity or pleasure of the senses that draws us here, but firm faith and ardent hope and sincere love.

THE IMITATION OF CHRIST, THOMAS À KEMPIS, BOOK 4, PART 1

Prayers of Intercession

To the Lord, let us pray:

Guide the course of events so that your Church may have the freedom to bring salvation to people everywhere.

Grant our Holy Father, the Pope, good health and wisdom so that he may lead God's people.

Assist our bishops, priests, and deacons to do your work more perfectly, to increase our faith, and to make us more discerning and more loving followers of Christ.

Shepherd all those preparing for baptism, forgive their sins in the waters of new life, and grant them a new beginning in Jesus Christ our Lord.

Gather together in one Church all those who share our faith in Jesus Christ.

Enlighten those who do not believe in Christ and show them the path to salvation through the grace of the Holy Spirit.

Watch over all those in public office and inspire their
hearts and minds so that peace and freedom may reign
in this world.

Give special attention to all those in need—the sick, the
dying, the unjustly imprisoned, and rid the world of
falsehood, hunger, poverty, and disease.

We ask all this through Christ our Lord. Amen.

ADAPTED FROM THE LITURGY OF THE WORD FOR GOOD FRIDAY

Litany of Praise of the Most Precious Blood of Jesus

Lord, have mercy on us. *Christ, have mercy on us.*

Lord, have mercy on us. Christ, hear us. *Christ graciously
hear us.*

God, the Father of Heaven, *have mercy on us.*

God, the Son, Redeemer of the world, *have mercy on us.*

Holy Trinity, One God, *have mercy on us.*

Blood of Christ, only begotten Son of the Eternal Father,
save us.

Blood of Christ, of the New and Eternal Testament,
save us.

Blood of Christ, falling upon the earth in the Agony,
save us.

Blood of Christ, flowing forth in the Crowning with
Thorns, *save us.*

Blood of Christ, poured out on the Cross, *save us.*

Blood of Christ, price of our salvation, *save us.*

Blood of Christ, without which there is no forgiveness,
save us.

Blood of Christ, eucharistic drink and refreshment
of souls, *save us.*

Blood of Christ, river of mercy, *save us.*

Blood of Christ, victor over demons, *save us.*
Blood of Christ, courage of martyrs, *save us.*
Blood of Christ, strength of confessors, *save us.*
Blood of Christ, bringing forth virgins, *save us.*
Blood of Christ, help of those in peril, *save us.*
Blood of Christ, relief of the burdened, *save us.*
Blood of Christ, solace in sorrow, *save us.*
Blood of Christ, hope of the penitent, *save us.*
Blood of Christ, consolation of the dying, *save us.*
Blood of Christ, peace and tenderness of hearts, *save us.*
Blood of Christ, pledge of eternal life, *save us.*
Blood of Christ, freeing souls from purgatory, *save us.*
Blood of Christ, most worthy of all glory and honor,
    save us.

Lamb of God, who takes away the sins of the world,
    spare us, O Lord.
Lamb of God, who takes away the sins of the world,
    graciously hear us, O Lord.
Lamb of God, who takes away the sins of the world,
    have mercy on us.

Let us pray: Almighty and eternal God, you have appointed
your only-begotten Son the Redeemer of the world, and willed
to be appeased by his Blood, grant, we ask of you, that we
may worthily adore this Price of Our Salvation, and through
its power be safeguarded from the evils of this present life, so
that we may rejoice in its fruits forever in heaven. Through
the same Christ our Lord. Amen.

How to Pray a Holy Hour

The practice of a regular, or even daily, visit to the Blessed Sacrament is receiving renewed interest in the United States, especially because of the increased number of opportunities for Perpetual Adoration in many churches and dioceses and an increased attention to the doctrine of the Real Presence of Christ in the Blessed Sacrament.

One person most responsible for popularizing the practice of prayer before the Blessed Sacrament was Saint Alphonsus Liguori whose book *Visits to the Blessed Sacrament* has been in print since 1745. Each visit (in his book, Alphonsus provides an appropriate visit for each day of the month) consists of an opening prayer, a meditation on the Eucharist, a prayer of spiritual communion, a visit to the Blessed Mother, and, finally, a closing prayer.

Saint Alphonsus gives these suggestions for a visit to the Blessed Sacrament:

- After entering the church or chapel in which the Blessed Sacrament is reserved or exposed, mentally place yourself in the presence of Jesus in the Blessed Sacrament.

- Enter into a conversation with Christ present before you just as you would talk with a trusted friend.

- Pray for forgiveness of your sins and help in correcting your faults.

- Tell Jesus the things that are bothering you, the obstacles in your journey of salvation. Share with him your needs and those for whom you are praying.

- Ask Jesus to grant you greater love of him.

- Continue praying prayers of praise, thanksgiving, and love while in his eucharistic presence.

A Visit to the Blessed Sacrament by Saint Alphonsus Liguori

Here is an example of the visit to the Blessed Sacrament as written by Saint Alphonsus Liguori. Some of the sentences have been shortened and simplified.

Introductory Prayer

My Lord Jesus Christ, I believe that you are really here in this sacrament. Night and day you remain here, compassionate and loving. You call, you wait for, you welcome, everyone who comes to visit you.

Unimportant though I am, I adore you. I thank you for all the wonderful graces you have given me. But I thank you especially for having given me yourself in this sacrament, for having asked your own Mother to mother me, for having called me here to talk to you.

I am here before you today to do three things: to thank you for these precious gifts, to make up for all the disrespect that you receive in this sacrament from those who offend you, to adore you everywhere in the world where you are present in this living bread but are left abandoned and unloved.

My Jesus, I love you with all my heart. I know I have displeased you often in the past—I am sorry. With your help I promise never to do it again. I am only a miserable sinner, but I consecrate myself to you completely. I give you my will, my love, my desires, everything I own. From now on do what you please with me. All I ask is that you love me, that you keep me faithful to the end of my life. I ask for the grace to do your will exactly as you want it done.

I pray for the souls in purgatory—especially for those who were close to you in this sacrament and close to your Mother Mary. I pray for every soul hardened in sin. My Savior, I unite my love to the love of your divine heart, and I offer them both together to your Father. I beg him to accept this offering in your name. Amen.

Meditation on the Holy Eucharist

A certain holy priest liked to think of Christ in the Blessed Sacrament with his arms loaded with graces, waiting to give them away. Here I am, Lord, ready to receive them.

My God, I realize that you deserve to be loved more than anything else in the world. I want to love you as profoundly as the human heart can love. But, traitor and rebel that I am, I am not entitled to this love. I am not worthy to kneel here before you. Yet you ask us to love: *My sons and daughters, give me your hearts.* You command us: *Love the Lord with all your heart.* I really believe this is why you have spared my life: to give me another chance to love you.

Since this is the way you want it, Lord, I yield to your request and command. I offer myself to you; I love you. Only you can cultivate my barren heart. It is a cold, cramped, calloused heart; but since you ask for it, it is yours. Surely if you accept it, you will rid it of all selfishness.

Change me, Lord! By ignoring you, I have been extremely ungrateful. Your boundless goodness deserves boundless love. Starting right now, let me make up for all the love I have held back in the past.

Act of Spiritual Communion

My Jesus, I believe you are really here in the Blessed Sacrament. I love you more than anything in the world, and I hunger to feed on your flesh. But since I cannot receive Communion at this moment, feed my soul at least spiritually. I unite myself to you now as I do when I actually receive you. Never let me drift away from you.

Visit With Mary

Mary is like Jesus in many ways. Because she is the Mother of Mercy, she is glad to help and comfort stumbling sinners. In fact, she is so eager to fill souls with choice graces that a holy man once said: "This Mother is more anxious to help us with her graces than we are anxious to receive them." O Mary, you are our hope.

Concluding Prayer

Most Holy Immaculate Virgin and my Mother Mary, to you who are the Mother of my Lord, the Queen of the world, the Advocate, the Hope, the Refuge of sinners, I have recourse today—I, who am the most miserable of all. I render you my most humble homage, O great Queen, and I thank you for all the graces you have conferred on me until now, particularly for having delivered me from hell, which I have so often deserved. I love you, O most amiable Lady; and for the love which I bear you, I promise to serve you always and to do all in my power to make others also love you. I place in you all my hopes; I confide my salvation to your care. Accept me for your servant and receive me under your mantle, O Mother of Mercy. And since you are so powerful with God, deliver me from all temptations, or rather obtain for me the strength to triumph over them until death. Of you I ask a perfect love for Jesus Christ. From you I hope to die a good death. O my Mother, by the love which you bear to God, I beseech you to help me at all times, but especially at the last moment of my life. Leave me not, I beseech you, until you see me safe in heaven, blessing you and singing your mercies for all eternity.

Amen. So I hope. So may it be.

Suggested Ways to Focus Your Prayer on a Visit to the Blessed Sacrament

Recount your failures to him. Ask him for help in eradicating them. Make sure to ask him to help in revealing those failure you do not want to acknowledge.

Pray for healing to the eucharistic Jesus: our physician, our strength, our savior.

Pray to know your own vocation in life. Pray for vocations to the priesthood and religious life.

Renew your baptismal vows.

Meditate on the sacred events of the life of Christ on earth: Incarnation, birth, public ministry, institution of the Holy Eucharist, agony in the Garden, arrest and condemnation, death, and Resurrection.

Read a life of Christ very slowly. Stop and meditate when a passage "speaks" to you. Ask your pastor or spiritual advisor to suggest an appropriate selection.

Pray for those who have hurt you. Ask Jesus to grant you true reconciliation.

Make a list of all the things for which you can be grateful. Thank him for his blessings.

Join in prayer for the dying throughout the world.

Decide on an appropriate gift for him and prepare a plan for its accomplishment.

Meditate on the virtues of Jesus according to the day of the week: Sunday: the love he bears his Father; Monday: the love he bears to us; Tuesday: his obedience to his Father; Wednesday: his humility; Thursday: his poverty; Friday: his patience; Saturday: the resignation with which he accepts the will of the Father.

Read Sacred Scripture slowly and thoughtfully. Stop when a particular image or passage attracts your attention. Listen to the words of Scripture. Listen to Our Lord speaking to you through those words.

Find a book on Centering Prayer and undertake it during these visits to the Blessed Sacrament.

Assure him that you love him.

Prayers for a Private Visit to the Blessed Sacrament

Here is a selection of prayers suitable for a private visit to the Blessed Sacrament. You may also wish to use these prayers as a model to create prayers of your own.

The Angel's Prayer at Fátima

Most Holy Trinity—Father, Son, and Holy Spirit—I adore you from the depths of my being. I offer you the body, blood, soul, and divinity of Jesus Christ, present in all the tabernacles of the world, in reparation for the outrages, sacrileges, and indifferences by which he is offended. And through the infinite merits of his most Sacred Heart and the Immaculate Heart of Mary, I ask of you the conversion of all sinners. Amen.

Prayer of Saint Faustina Kowalski

I adore you, Lord and Creator, hidden in the Most Blessed Sacrament. I adore you for all the works of your hands that reveal to me so much wisdom, goodness, and mercy, O Lord. You have spread so much beauty over the earth and it tells me about your beauty, even though these things are but a faint reflection of your incomprehensible attraction. And though you have hidden yourself and concealed your beauty, my eye, enlightened by faith, reaches you, and my soul recognizes its creator, its highest good.

My Lord, your goodness encourages me to converse with you. Your mercy abolishes the chasm which separates the creator from the creature. You, O Lord, are the delight of my heart. Amen.

Prayer of Nicolas of Cusa

O Lord, how sweet is your goodness. It is your will that we proclaim your death in the eating of the Bread of Life. What more could you give to us, who deserve to die through the eating of the forbidden fruit than life through the eating of the Bread? O Food of Life, nailed to the Cross, who can grasp the bountiful gift which you offer—the gift of your very self as food?

O Food which truly nourishes and satisfies, not our flesh but our soul, not our body but our spirit. O Memorial, worthy to be cherished in our inmost soul, to be deeply engraved on our mind, and lovingly preserved in the tabernacle of our heart. Its remembrance is a joy forever, and a cause for tears that well up from a heart filled with overpowering joy. Amen.

Prayer of Saint John Chrysostom

O Lord, bless those who bless you, and sanctify those who trust in you, save your people and bless their inheritance, and keep your household, the Church, under your protection. Sanctify those who love the beauty of your house; reward them with glory through your divine power; and do not forsake those who hope in you. To the sick give your aid, healing, and comfort. Keep safe all who travel by land or water. Send us seasonable weather and bless the fruits of the earth. Keep peace in the world, and among all your people.

Grant rest to the departed, and remember those who have offered gifts to you. Save those who are in any way afflicted or distressed, and grant us all your heavenly grace. Amen.

Prayer of Pope John XXIII

O Jesus, King of all peoples and all ages, accept the acts of adoration and praise which we, your sisters and brothers by adoption, humbly offer you.

You are the "living Bread which comes down from heaven and gives life to the world" (Jn 6:33), Supreme Priest and Victim. On the Cross you offered yourself to the Eternal Father as a bloody sacrifice of expiation, for the redemption of the human race, and now you offer yourself daily upon our altars by the hands of your ministers, in order to establish in every heart your "reign of truth and life, of holiness and grace, of justice, love and peace" (Preface of the Mass of Christ the King).

O King of glory, may your kingdom come! Reign from your "throne of grace" (Heb 4:14), in our homes, so that parents and children may live in peace in obedience to your holy law. Reign in our land, so that all citizens, in the harmonious order of the various social groups, may feel themselves children of the same heavenly Father, called to cooperate for the common good of this world, happy to belong to the one Mystical Body, of which your sacrament is at once the symbol and everlasting source.

O Jesus, present in the sacrament of the altar, teach all the nations to serve you with willing hearts, knowing that "to serve God is to reign." May your sacrament, O Jesus, be light to the mind, strength to the will, joy to the heart. May it be the support of the weak, the comfort of the suffering, the wayfaring bread of salvation for the dying, and for all the "pledge of future glory." Amen.

Short Prayers

Jesus, our unfailing source of goodness, friend of our souls, let our prayers knock at your tabernacle door, begging you to open to us, to welcome us and through your Blessed Sacrament bring to us a favorable answer to every sacred desire of our hearts, through the help of your grace. Amen.

Heart of Jesus, made for love of us, living for love of us, dying for love of us, be always our good friend, consoling us when we visit you, blessing us in your Holy Eucharist, and giving yourself to us in Holy Communion, so that our hearts, inspired by your great love, may grow in devotion to you, now and to the hour of our deaths. Amen.

May the heart of Jesus in the Most Blessed Sacrament be praised, adored, and loved with grateful affection, at every moment, in all the tabernacles of the world, even to the end of time. Amen.

O Lord, drop into my heart but a spark of the love which raged in your blood. Grant to me some of that affection which burned within you. Mother and father and children love one another because the same blood flows in their veins, but your blood, my Savior, flows into my very soul, saving it. Intense then should be the fire which burns within me; higher should its flames ascend than in any earthly love. Blood of Christ, inflame with love of you. Amen.